From Dreams to Reality
Career Cards

Girl Scouts of the U.S.A.
830 Third Avenue
New York, N.Y. 10022

 GIRL SCOUTS OF THE U.S.A.

Betty F. Pilsbury, *President*
Frances Hesselbein, *National Executive Director*

Inquiries related to *From Dreams to Reality* should be addressed to the Program Department, Girl Scouts of the U.S.A., 830 Third Avenue, New York, N.Y. 10022.

From Dreams to Reality: Career Cards
Conceived by: Roxanne Spillett
Authors: Roxanne Spillett, Mary Gilmore, Nancy Garfield
Project Director: Nancy Garfield

Most of the sections of this work were developed under a grant from the United States Office of Education, Department of Health, Education, and Welfare. However, the content does not necessarily reflect the position or policy of that Agency and no official endorsement of these materials should be inferred.

All rights reserved
First Impression 1978, Second Printing December 1984
Printed in the United States of America
Girl Scout Catalog No. 20-818
ISBN 0-88441-335-7
5 4

Contents

The World of Well-Being
Clergywoman 1
Clinical Psychologist 3
Dentist 5
Dietitian 7
Health Administrator 9
Lifeguard 11
Medical Record Administrator 13
Nurse 15
Occupational Therapist 17
Orthotic and Prosthetic Technician 19
Parent 21
Physician 23
Police Officer 25
Respiratory Therapist 27
Social Worker 29
Veterinarian 31

The World of People
College Professor 33
Director of a Multicultural Affairs Organization 35
Early Childhood Supervisor 37
Economist 39
Fire Dispatcher 41
High School Teacher 43
Historian 45
Human Resources Administrator 47
Information Officer in the Armed Forces 49
International Program Officer 51
Lawyer 53
Political Scientist 55
Post Office Supervisor 57
Program Services Director 59
School Administrator 61
Sociologist 63

The World of Today and Tomorrow
Accountant 65
Anthropologist 67
Astronaut 69
Auto Mechanic 71
Carpenter 73
Computer Operator 75
Computer Programmer 77

Drafter	79
Electrician's Helper	81
Engineer	83
Flight Attendant	85
Geologist	87
Insurance Salesperson	89
Marine Biologist	91
Stockbroker	93
Telephone Installer	95

The World of the Arts

Actress	97
Architect	99
Art Director	101
Ceramicist	103
Conductor	105
Dancer	107
Fashion Designer	109
Foreign Correspondent	111
Illustrator	113
Interior Designer	115
Journalist-Editor	117
Musician	119
Photographer	121
Playwright	123
Producer	125
Puppeteer	127

The World of the Out-of-Doors

Athlete	129
Athletic Director	131
Athletic Trainer	133
Camp Director	135
Coach	137
Forester	139
Horse Trainer	141
Horticulturist	143
Meteorologist	145
Naturalist	147
Park Administrator	149
Recreation Leader	151
Recreation Specialist	153
Soil Scientist	155
Sportswriter	157
Zookeeper	159
Blank Career Cards	161

Clergywoman

Well-Being

"Parish ministry? It's not something people thought a woman would ever do. I don't ever remember wanting to be a minister," says Arabella Meadows-Rogers. But Arabella decided to enter a seminary after college because she wanted to work with people and she had an interest in religion. There she met other women who were learning that they had talents and abilities that could be used in the ministry. Today, Arabella is one of three ministers of a beautiful red sandstone church that is over 75 years old.

At first, Arabella took the position because it was, conveniently, in the city where she had studied and close enough to her husband's church. (He is a minister, too.) Now, Arabella is committed to urban ministry. "What I love about this church is the incredible conglomeration of people who come here—rich, poor, singles, families, every ethnic group. And the best part is they all run the church together."

In addition to conducting services, counseling, and visiting the sick and the homebound, Arabella works with committees made up of church members to deal with community problems and contact local legislators. These committees also work with other community agencies to help solve the problems of urban life.

For Arabella, one of the exciting aspects of her job is that she can make it what she'd like it to be. There's room to bring her special interests and ideas into her work. Yet, the ministry is far from a quiet life. A lot is expected of Arabella, and she makes every effort to do her best.

Arabella would like to have a church of her own one day. As a woman, she feels pretty much "on show" right now, but she believes more women will enter the ministry in the future. If you are considering a career in the ministry, Arabella recommends keeping a close contact with your church or synagogue, being involved in human problems, and getting to know yourself so that you can best help others.

Clergywoman

All religious clergy have a similar responsibility—to serve the spiritual, ethical, and religious needs of their congregations. All possess a strong religious faith and a desire to help others. Ministers, priests, and rabbis administer religious rites; deliver spiritual messages; conduct religious services; give religious instruction; and counsel people who are ill, lonely, or in search of guidance. Religious leaders also may engage in interfaith, community, civic, recreational, and educational activities.

Special Qualities

interested in serving others
religious
moral
sensitive
scholarly
skilled in oral communication
tactful

Education and Training

Educational requirements for entry into the clergy vary all the way from no formal educational requirements to extensive courses of study following college graduation.

Salary Range

$6,000–$75,000
(Salaries vary widely depending on the religious order and whether allowances are given for housing and other personal expenses such as food, clothing, and education.)

Places of Employment

churches and synagogues
theological seminaries
social service organizations
hospitals
Armed Forces
colleges and universities

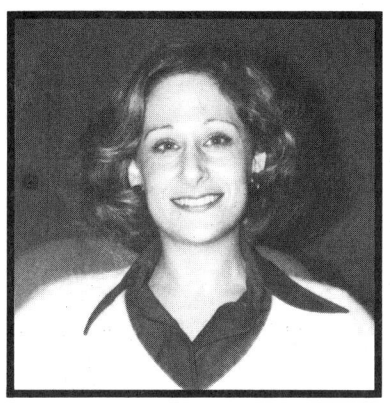

Clinical Psychologist

Well-Being

"The most exciting thing about my career is seeing people grow and develop," claims Dr. Marla Silverman, clinical psychologist. For Marla, psychotherapy provides a way for people to deal with the problems and conflicts in their lives and learn to cope with them or change their life situations for the better.

Marla wanted to do something that would be very challenging with little routine and repetition and she's sure she found it in clinical psychology. She works three days a week, seeing six to eight people a day. She counsels people individually, in couples, and in groups. When she is not seeing patients, Marla is busy scheduling appointments, talking to her patients on the telephone, filling out records and insurance forms, and exchanging professional insights with colleagues.

Someday Marla may professionally supervise other psychologists or collaborate on writing a book on creativity. For now, she is very satisfied seeing private patients and she is excited about having her own office. Marla also feels private practice will fit well with her plans to raise a family.

Marla encourages young women to consider the field of clinical psychology—a field which offers both opportunity and challenge. "For this career," she explains, "you should be sensitive to how you and other people are thinking and feeling and try to heighten your own powers of awareness. It's important to respect both the strengths and defenses of people." But no matter what career you choose, Marla has some advice. "Don't decide on a career that other people have chosen for you. Trust your interests and use lots of creativity in pursuing your goals."

3

Clinical Psychologist

A clinical psychologist works closely and directly with people to help them resolve the personal problems that may be preventing them from achieving their potential. The psychologist may work with mildly upset or more severely disturbed people. She/he interviews and counsels patients; gives diagnostic tests; and provides individual, family, and group psychotherapy. Research, teaching, or supervising other psychologists are other functions of a clinical psychologist.

Special Qualities

emotionally stable
mature
sensitive
able to relate to people
patient
curious about human behavior

Education and Training

A bachelor's degree plus a master's degree and a doctorate are becoming increasingly important for high-level positions and for establishing a private practice. In addition, a psychologist generally needs to be licensed, or certified, to work in her/his state.

Salary Range

$27,000–$50,000+

Places of Employment

private practice
hospitals
clinics
schools, colleges, and universities
research centers

Dentist

Well-Being

After college graduation, when many of her friends were earning dollars, Helen Burrell was studying hard without pay. Then, when the summer came and her friends were vacationing, Helen continued to study hard. "A dental education is long and costly and you must be prepared to make that sacrifice," Helen explains. "But in the end, it's all worthwhile."

Helen (officially Dr. Burrell) is now a dentist who specializes in orthodontics (straightening teeth). In her practice, a typical day begins at 10:00 A.M. and ends at 6:00 P.M., with 15 patients in between. In addition to placing wires and bands on her patients' teeth, there are X-rays and photographs to be taken and impressions (models) to be made. All of this, explains Dr. Burrell, helps her analyze her patients' problems, plan their treatment, and measure their progress.

Achieving progress is a number-one reward for Helen, not to mention the patient! She explains that straightening teeth often improves a person's appearance and can be a tremendous psychological lift.

Because she has a practice of her own, Helen has the added responsibility of overseeing the business operations of her office. And, in her already busy day, that often means staying after hours and missing out on some social activities every now and then. But, as Helen explains, "My patients come first."

Dr. Burrell, who was introduced to her career by a family dentist, has some helpful words for anyone considering dentistry as a career. "The best things in life aren't free," she says about the ten years of hard work she invested in preparing for her career. As she happily concludes, "I love my practice!"

Copyright ©1978 Girl Scouts of the United States of America

Dentist

A dentist examines, treats, and tries to prevent diseases and disorders of the gums and teeth. She/he fills cavities, extracts and replaces teeth, and may take X-rays. While most dentists are general practitioners providing all sorts of dental care, many others are specialists. For example, an orthodontist straightens teeth; a periodontist treats gum diseases; an oral surgeon operates on the mouth and jaw; and a pedodontist works only with children. In any case, the dentist may work with a team of other health professionals to provide the needed dental care.

Special Qualities

able to work well with hands
interested in science
able to judge space and shape well
business-minded
patient
understanding

Education and Training

Two to four years of college followed by four years of dental school are required. Additional study is necessary to specialize.

Salary Range

$59,000–$100,000+

Places of Employment

private practice
clinics
hospitals
dental schools

Dietitian

Well-Being

As chief dietitian in a large hospital, Julia Robinson is responsible for seeing that all patients receive the proper foods and that their meals are prepared and served in the best possible way. And that's a big responsibility. Big enough to require a staff of 80 from dietitians to chefs to cooks!

To manage a job this big, and still have time for lunch, Julia has a routine. In the morning she meets with her staff to check out any problems and discuss solutions; for example, the patient whose low-salt diet calls for a certain kind of cereal that isn't available, or the patient who didn't receive a tray. Then Julia makes rounds, visiting 15 or 20 patients at random to learn how satisfactory their meals have been. The afternoon is not so structured. She visits with salespeople, meets with families of patients, does testing to determine the quality of food, and handles staff-related tasks like scheduling hours.

Although much of her responsibility is supervising a large staff, Julia gets most satisfaction from the patients themselves. When an ill person returns home, partially as a result of the work she has done, she sees it as "a real contribution to society." She recalls one young patient who refused to eat. Julia worked closely with a psychiatrist to make sure the patient got the emotional support and the nutrition she needed. When the patient regained her health, both physically and emotionally, Julia felt very rewarded.

She's disappointed, on the other hand, when patients aren't given the tender loving care they need. According to Julia, "If patients are hostile, they have a reason." Julia sees compassion and understanding as essentials for health-care jobs.

Julia has some advice for anyone interested in a career as a dietitian. "While you're still in high school, be sure to take science courses. And before you select a college, talk to your guidance counselor about an approved program."

Dietitian

A dietitian is a specialist who applies the science of nutrition and management to help people select foods that will nourish their bodies in health and sickness throughout their lives. A dietitian may also supervise all aspects of food service management, teach food and nutrition principles, and counsel people concerning diet.

Special Qualities
able to work well with others
interested in studying foods and nutrition
organized
interested in management

Education and Training
A bachelor's degree in dietetics, nutrition, food science, or food service management, plus some clinical experience, are required.

Salary Range
$20,400–$30,000

Places of Employment
hospitals
public health agencies
schools, colleges, and universities
military installations
commercial food services

Health Administrator

Well-Being

For a girl who had a great deal of difficulty deciding on a college major and even more when it came to choosing a career, Ann Allen-Ryan has little trouble making decisions today. As assistant vice president of a major medical center, Ann is involved in near constant policy-making and management decisions.

As she goes about her daily business of running a hospital, Ann has developed her own style of administration. Although the job requires a lot of paperwork, she prefers getting around and meeting people. "Administration is more than sitting behind a desk, shuffling papers, and signing my name," she says. A good part of her day is spent on patient floors meeting with department heads. In addition, she attends regularly scheduled board meetings, committee meetings, and staff meetings. Ann claims that in this way hospital problems are more readily solved, and the staff morale remains high.

Running an institution as large and complex as a hospital, Ann hasn't lost the human touch. For her, taking time out for small favors is particularly rewarding. She recalls the time she bent hospital rules to allow a young child to visit his sick mother. But Ann explains, "A hospital administrator is not just a superpowerful social worker." She believes the job requires toughmindedness, and most of all good business sense—especially when it comes to balancing a budget.

If you're the kind of person who enjoys making things work, if you like to take a problem area and analyze and reorganize it, or if you like to plan for the future and improve systems, Ann suggests looking into administration.

Now in a number-two position, Ann enjoys her job. Yet she is looking toward a change. When asked about her future plans, she smiles and says, "There's only one place to go from here—a number-one position."

Copyright © 1978 Girl Scouts of the United States of America

Health Administrator

Like the school principal, the administrator of a hospital or other health facility is in charge of the institution. She/he coordinates the efforts of all hospital departments to provide high-quality patient care. The job involves managing the hospital's personnel, equipment, and finances, as well as the building itself. Preparing and administering the budget in order to meet current and future health needs of the community is also part of the health administrator's job.

Special Qualities

able to organize and direct the work of others
skilled in oral communication
interested in community service
business-minded

Education and Training

A bachelor's degree in a related field and two years of graduate study in health administration are required.

Salary Range

$20,000–$60,000

Places of Employment

hospitals
health departments
nursing homes
clinics

Lifeguard

Well-Being

Ask anyone where they grew up and they'll probably tell you the name of a village, town, or city—no matter how small. But ask Joan Tynan this question and her answer may surprise you.

"I grew up in the water," Joan casually says of her childhood. (She has 60 trophies to prove it!) Swimming was always a major part of Joan's life. At six years old she was learning to swim at the Y. At eight, she was competing. At 14, she became a Junior Life Saver. At 16, she was a Senior Life Saver and a bona fide, employed lifeguard.

Since her first job, Joan has enjoyed several others. Because she resides in the northern part of the country, she usually works at shore clubs and beaches in the summer months and at indoor pools as the weather cools. No matter where she works, however, the routine is basically the same. On duty, she enforces pool safety rules and oversees swimming activity. (Although teaching is not required on the job, it's the part she particularly enjoys.)

When asked about her life-saving record, Joan says, "To tell the truth, I've been lucky." In her six-year career as a lifeguard there have been only five times she's had to "pull someone out," and only one really close call. About these times, Joan says, "I can see the panic in their faces." She adds with assurance, "I know what has to be done, and I do it—fast."

Joan reminds young people interested in a similar career that lifeguarding is a "hard job with heavy responsibilities." According to her, to do this job well you must be physically fit, be able to concentrate, and have a strong sense of responsibility. As a start, she suggests enrolling in a lifesaving course. After all, that's how Joan got started.

Lifeguard

A lifeguard oversees a swimming area to prevent accidents. In addition to rescuing swimmers and administering first aid, the lifeguard enforces pool safety rules, advises swimmers about unsafe areas, and inspects the water for cleanliness.

Special Qualities

physically fit
responsible
able to concentrate for long periods of time
skilled in swimming

Education and Training

An advanced Life Saving Certificate from the American National Red Cross, or an equivalent from the YMCA or Boy Scouts of America is required. To direct waterfront activities such as boating or swimming instruction, a candidate needs a Water Safety Instructor Certificate.

Salary Range

A lifeguard is usually paid by the hour, starting at the minimum wage. The pay increases with experience.

Places of Employment

beaches
shore and country clubs
recreation centers
public and private pools
schools
health clubs
camps

Medical Record Administrator

Well-Being

As a young girl, all Nellie Presley could think about was nursing. But after realizing she didn't particularly enjoy being around sick people and hated the sight of blood, her career dream abruptly ended.

Today, as director of medical records in a small hospital, Nellie strikes a compromise. She keeps close ties with medicine, yet maintains a distance from sick patients. Patients or not, according to Nellie "there's never a dull moment" in the record-keeping division of a hospital. As she explains, "With incomplete medical records to be handled, there's always something to do." Completing a record usually involves a lot of letter writing and legwork as she tracks down the missing medical reports. Besides these records, there are conferences to attend, statistical reports to be compiled, requests for information to be filled, and charts to be filed.

Because Nellie is a highly organized person, she gets a feeling of accomplishment when she completes even one patient's chart. And, of course, real frustration results when information is nowhere to be found and when an occasional medical record is missing entirely.

If you're thinking of a career in medical records, Nellie suggests you volunteer or work part-time in the medical records department of a hospital. She also warns that "some people may find this a boring profession." But she adds, "If you like to see everything orderly, organized, and in its place, and you enjoy working with physicians, this field can be extremely gratifying."

Medical Record Administrator

The medical record administrator develops the hospital's system for gathering reports for a patient's complete medical record, analyzing the content of medical records for statistical reports, storing medical records for future use, and retrieving medical records. The administrator is assisted by a staff of medical record technicians to help this system operate smoothly.

Special Qualities
accurate
skilled in oral and written communication
precise
detail-minded
organized
patient

Education and Training
For a medical record administrator, a bachelor's degree in medical record administration is required. For a medical record technician, a ten-month certificate program or an associate's degree is required.

Salary Range
Medical Record Administrator: $15,000–$35,000
Medical Record Technician: $13,300–$25,000

Places of Employment
hospitals
clinics
nursing homes
health departments
research facilities

Nurse

Well-Being

Since she was a toddler, there was never any doubt in Chris Kelly's mind that she was going to be a nurse. What Chris Kelly didn't know at the time was just how far she would progress in the field.

During her first ten years as a registered nurse, Chris worked in the labor room and the nursery caring directly for patients and working her share of evening duty, night duty, and weekends. Then came her promotion to head nurse in the nursery for newborns. And as Chris gained more experience, she moved on to supervise the entire obstetrics department, directing a staff of 30. Then came the big promotion to supervisor where her job was to oversee the work of the hospital staff in six departments. In this position, Chris had the responsibility for 150 patients. "You have to have mighty broad shoulders," says Chris about the responsibility she felt.

Despite the high position, though, Chris was not altogether happy. "I'm not a disciplinarian," she confides. So Chris moved out of her supervisory role into her present position as instructor in the staff development department where she is responsible for the orientation of all new nursing personnel. In this role, Chris feels she has the best of many worlds. She still has contact with patients, yet she serves as a consultant to the nursing staff for their educational needs and she has the opportunity to teach, too.

For someone who was once told that she wouldn't make it in the nursing field because she was "too friendly," Chris has climbed a long way up the health career ladder. But there were no shortcuts. Only education and experience and more education and experience—and lots of patience along the way. Will this woman-on-the-move settle into a lifetime position in staff development? Chris smiles and says, "Only time will tell."

Copyright © 1978 Girl Scouts of the United States of America

Nurse

In a hospital, a nurse is part of the health care team working with patients of all types. The registered professional nurse is the planner of a patient's nursing care. She/he cares for the ill, trains patients and their families to take part in the patient's therapy, and supervises other nursing personnel. The licensed practical nurse or vocational nurse assists with the care of selected patients. Nurses also work in community health agencies promoting and providing health care for the residents. These nurses may give special treatments to the chronically ill, teach new mothers how to care for their babies, do health assessments, teach, and aid the handicapped.

Special Qualities

able to handle emergency situations
reliable
interested in working with people
emotionally stable
alert
able to use good judgment
sympathetic to the needs of others

Education and Training

For a registered nurse, a two-year associate's degree, a bachelor's degree, or a hospital-based diploma program (two to three years) is required. For a licensed practical nurse, one year of training in a vocational program or hospital is needed.

Salary Range

Registered Nurse: $20,400–$42,200
Licensed Practical Nurse: $13,000–$19,900

Places of Employment

hospitals
nursing homes
government health departments
community health agencies
industries
schools
doctors' offices
private homes
self-employment

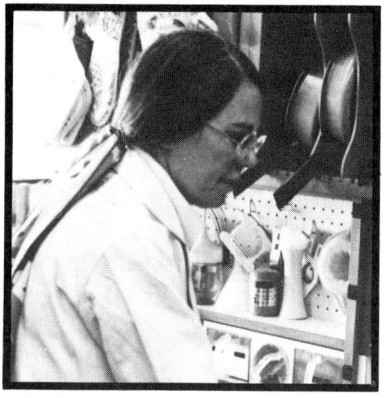

Occupational Therapist

Well-Being

A letter from a friend introduced Mercedes Abella to a career in occupational therapy. "There's this job that's just right for you," it began. Mercedes decided to look into it.

Today, Mercedes is assistant director of an occupational therapy department in a rehabilitation center where her responsibilities are largely administrative. But she recalls her first 21 years as an occupational therapist very well. She worked with about eight patients each day, and, in addition, attended conferences and prepared reports. In the course of her career she has helped many physically disabled people learn to care for themselves and find their place in the working world.

Speaking about her present job, she says, "If the day had 48 hours, I could accomplish all I want." But as busy as Mercedes is as an administrator, she misses the patient contact. She has found that "with upward mobility, you lose touch with patients." Yet, the many letters, phone calls, and return visits from former patients continually remind her of the rewards in patient care.

But some cases did not work out as she hoped. For example, she recalls a young boy, an accident victim, whom she worked with until he was practically independent again. He could feed, dress, and transfer himself. Yet, he couldn't return to school because there were no ramps or other facilities for the handicapped.

Mercedes brings a strong sense of commitment to her work. "When you deal with human beings, you must do all you can, the best you can." For the aspiring occupational therapist, she adds, "Success means never losing your human touch."

Occupational Therapist

Through a planned program of purposeful activities requiring physical and mental involvement of the patient, the occupational therapist, together with other members of the rehabilitation team, helps physically disabled and emotionally disturbed people care for themselves. The occupational therapist must first evaluate her/his patient by means of observation and testing. Then, based on these findings, she/he will plan a program of activities that will help the handicapped master job-related skills and exercises for daily living.

Special Qualities

concerned for the disabled
warm
patient
responsible
determined
able to relate to people
creative
organized

Education and Training

For a registered occupational therapist, a bachelor's degree and at least six months of practical experience are required. For an occupational therapy assistant, a one- or two-year occupational therapy assistant's program is needed.

Salary Range

Occupational Therapist: $21,000–$26,000
Occupational Therapy Assistant: $9,000–$18,000

Places of Employment

hospitals
rehabilitation centers
nursing homes
private homes

Orthotic and Prosthetic Technician

Well-Being

Joanne Klope is an orthotic and prosthetic technician, and if you're like everyone else you'll undoubtedly ask, "What's that?"

Actually, Joanne makes artificial limbs and braces. "People don't know this field exists," she observes. "They must think these devices fall from the sky." Yet, each day Joanne spends hours at her workbench, fabricating artificial arms, legs, and hands. When she is not in the lab making these devices, she is consulting with physicians or, more often, meeting directly with patients for fittings.

In a job that seems so technical, Joanne finds a great deal of reward in whatever patient contact she has. From the very first measurements to the final fitting, she may see a patient three to five times. As Joanne explains, "It's a very positive feeling to see an individual without a limb stand on his own two legs again."

But witnessing "the completion of a person" isn't always enough. Joanne tells the story of a young surfer who lost both arms in an accident. Although she knows her devices helped make him whole again, she also realizes that "he'll never fully return to the things he loves most."

Joanne feels comfortable in a field traditionally dominated by men. Although some people doubt her ability to work with complex machinery and tools, many more recognize the importance of a woman technician working with female patients. In Joanne's words, "I feel I'm in the right place at the right time." In fact, she has plans of owning and operating an orthotic and prosthetic facility of her own someday.

Orthotic and Prosthetic Technician

The orthotic and prosthetic technician makes and often helps fit artificial limbs and braces. The technician assists both the prosthetist (who designs artificial limbs) and the orthotist (who designs braces to correct physical defects). To make the devices as comfortable as possible, the orthotic and prosthetic technician works from a physician's description and will meet with a patient several times to make sure the device fits properly.

Special Qualities
concerned for the disabled
patient
accurate
able to work well with hands
mechanically minded

Education and Training
An orthotic and prosthetic technician may train on the job. For an orthotist or a prosthetist, a bachelor's degree with special training in orthotics or prosthetics will be required for all positions as of 1980.

Salary Range
Orthotic and Prosthetic Technician: $10,000–$18,000
Orthotist: $16,000–$32,000
Prosthetist: $16,000–$32,000

Places of Employment
hospitals
laboratories
rehabilitation centers

Parent

Well-Being

"Enjoy and participate in the growth of your children," urges Anna Gilmore, mother of six-year-old Steffie and four-year-old Peter.

Anna explains what she means. Before her children were born, she was a nurse-clinician in a hospital program where she treated children with hereditary diseases and counseled their parents. Then Steffie and Peter entered her life. Although she returned to work after each child was born, when budget cuts eliminated her job, her husband urged her to "move into full-time motherhood."

Anna feels that being with her preschool children is very important because her influence can be so crucial to their development. "I get the biggest thrill doing those things with them that I did as a child. I use every opportunity to teach my children about their world. As they grow, it's good to be with them to share their everyday experiences and joys."

Anna's typical day includes a family breakfast, a half-day of school for Peter and Steffie, lunch, afternoon activities (outdoor play, art, baking, games, having friends over), bath, dinner, story time, and bed for the children by 7:30 P.M. Somehow Anna manages to fit in shopping, cleaning, laundry, and volunteer activities. Evenings are Anna's to share with her husband, relax, read, or catch up on the many things she didn't get done during the day. Anna's volunteer work has helped her realize her additional talents besides nursing, motherhood, and housekeeping.

Although she will probably return to a paying job once her children are older, Anna says, "Full-time motherhood has been an extremely happy part of my life." She only wishes she had more time to spend with each child individually.

Anna's advice to prospective mothers? Go as far as you want in education. Then give yourself time to try your wings, and get to know yourself before you have your children. Being a mother takes a sensitive and well-rounded person.

Parent

Parents have the responsibility for the care, development, and protection of the children in a family. They may have given birth to these children, adopted them, or accepted them into their homes as foster children. Parents plan, supervise, and participate in their children's activities—play, mealtimes, schoolwork, religious activities, and hobbies. Parents also try to make sure that their children's activities outside the home are appropriate for their individual needs and abilities. Parenting requires sensitivity and patience to aid in children's social and emotional development and in caring for them during illness.

Special Qualities

patient
appreciative of children's abilities
able to use good judgment
resourceful
emotionally stable
able to coordinate family activities
interested in child development

Education and Training

Experience with children of a variety of ages is valuable training for young people planning to be parents.

Salary Range

Parents are rarely paid a salary. Many mothers and fathers have paying jobs in addition to their responsibilities as parents.

Places of Employment

Parents are responsible for their children in the home, in school, and in their community.

Physician

Well-Being

At the young age of five years, Jeanne Pamilla sat down and had a heart-to-heart talk with mother. The subject—a career. The choice—M.D. After high school, college, medical school, general surgical training, and three years of orthopedic surgical training, Jeanne not only earned the title of M.D., but is now a certified orthopedic surgeon as well.

For Dr. Pamilla, the day begins at 6:00 A.M. with hospital rounds. After seeing all her patients individually, she meets with other doctors for a conference at 7:30. The rest of the morning is spent treating patients in the clinic or operating room. (Dr. Pamilla performs from one to seven operations a day.) In the afternoon, the scenery changes as Jeanne leaves the hospital for her private practice across the street. Here she sees additional patients. Reflecting on her schedule, she sighs, "There just aren't enough hours in the day."

Despite the hurried pace, Jeanne enjoys her job—particularly performing surgery. She explains, "Even though there's pressure, lots of tension, and little room for error, a successful operation usually means immediate improvement for the patient and no delay of gratification for me."

As for being a female physician, Jeanne explains, smiling, "It's not unusual for a patient to ask me for a bedpan or to turn up the TV." Then, after learning she's a surgeon, there's the occasional patient who shrieks, "You mean she operates, too!"

But Jeanne is not easily discouraged. Some advice: "If there's something you want to do, and you feel competent—do it!" She recalls, "I've heard lots of discouraging advice. Had I listened, I wouldn't be here today."

Physician

A physician examines and treats patients to prevent or cure illness or injury. While a growing number of physicians are family practitioners, a physician may specialize in one of the 33 fields recognized by the medical profession. Some of the more common specialties are general surgery, pediatrics (care of children), psychiatry (study and treatment of disorders of the mind), and radiology (use of radiation for the diagnosis and treatment of diseases).

Special Qualities

concerned for the sick and the injured
able to make major decisions
emotionally stable
interested in science
sympathetic
understanding
sensitive
business-minded

Education and Training

A bachelor's degree plus four years of medical school are required to earn the M.D. degree. For specialization, an additional two to six years of training (residency) in a hospital are needed.

Salary Range

$20,000–$106,300+

Places of Employment

private practice
hospitals
research facilities
medical schools

Police Officer

Well-Being

Dressing up as a housewife in housecoat and hair rollers may seem like fun and games. But for Delores Johnson, undercover police officer, this charade was serious business.

In her 13 years on the force, Delores spent the first ten in the detective bureau, routinely following up on missing persons and auto accidents and working with female prisoners and juveniles.

With her promotion to sergeant, Delores now supervises a whole team of police officers. On an average eight-hour tour in a patrol car (alone), she will monitor some 75 to 100 calls and respond to only 10 or 20. Delores explains that the majority of them are service calls—someone needing oxygen or transportation to a hospital—and are normally handled by the officers in her charge. Supervisors like Delores generally respond to major calls such as burglary, robbery, fire, assault, or homicide to oversee the officers on her team.

Delores admits that a career as a police officer can be emotionally trying. "I've seen every kind of human tragedy—from family fights and parents who just don't care to drug addicts and delinquents." She adds, "There is so much about this job that can make you feel bad. You have to be able to take it." Delores also points out that shift work can be "hazardous to your health." Because her hours are always changing, she finds herself eating breakfast for dinner and dinner for breakfast.

What has compelled Delores to spend 13 years on the force, progressing from police officer to sergeant, with her eye now on a promotion to lieutenant? Part of the answer is that the career gives her a chance to serve others. Delores recalls one girl who was "picked up" for drugs. It was Delores who took the time to listen and talk to her, and to see that this girl got the help she so desperately needed. According to Delores, "A police officer can make a difference in a person's life, and that makes it all worthwhile!"

Police Officer

Police work ranges from controlling traffic to preventing and investigating crimes. In a small community department, a police officer has many different duties. In a large police department, an officer is usually assigned to a specific type of duty such as patrol or traffic duty, criminal investigation, or handwriting and fingerprint identification. Most newly recruited officers begin on patrol duty where they are assigned a section of the community. They may patrol the area alone or with another officer; on foot or in a police vehicle. Their job is to remain alert and respond to any unusual circumstances or safety hazards.

Special Qualities
honest
physically fit
able to use good judgment
able to get along with others
responsible

Education and Training
A high school diploma is the minimum requirement. However, many police departments now require some college training.

Salary Range
$21,000–$33,600

Places of Employment
local police departments

Respiratory Therapist

Well-Being

Not everyone reads the fine print in the classified section of the newspaper. But Sophia Preza is glad she did. It was here she learned of a hospital-based training program for respiratory therapists.

As a respiratory therapist, Sophia works as part of a team diagnosing and treating heart and lung disorders. After checking to see which patients are scheduled for treatments, Sophia goes about her day bringing equipment to their bedside, administering treatments, and occasionally doing lab tests. On an average day she may see seven patients, treating them each twice a day. Sophia explains that with each treatment there is "demanding, intimate patient contact."

"Basically, the pace is comfortable," says Sophia, "and there is time for an occasional cup of coffee. But you still have to be on your toes in case of emergencies." Sophia recalls the times she hears Code 99 (heart attack) over the hospital loudspeaker. "It's times like these when the pace picks up, and the pressure is really on." Regarding life-and-death situations, Sophia explains, "At first I didn't want to be exposed to it, but after a while you realize that with your help, the chances are better that a patient can make it." Of course, working as part of a team to bring about a full recovery is most rewarding. Unfortunately, however, situations don't work out this well every day.

Women considering this line of work may be put off by the thought of handling big, heavy equipment. But according to Sophia, racks and other modernized equipment ease the job. She adds, "In this business it's not strength but compassion that counts."

Respiratory Therapist

A respiratory therapist (formerly called an inhalation therapist) treats patients who have breathing problems. Following doctor's orders, she/he uses special equipment to administer treatments. Patients may have problems ranging from chronic asthma to heart failure, from drug overdoses to shock. In emergency situations, respiratory therapists are among the first medical specialists called to the scene.

Special Qualities

able to handle emergency situations
able to work on a team
able to follow instructions
able to solve mechanical problems

Education and Training

Preparation may vary from an 18-month certificate program to a four-year college degree program.

Salary Range

$17,800–$22,300

Places of Employment

hospitals
ambulance services
oxygen equipment rental companies
nursing homes

Social Worker

Well-Being

Ada Deer is a social worker making a difference. Like all other social workers, her goal is to improve the quality of life. Unlike some, however, she's able to use her energies to prevent problems before they begin.

Ada explains that there are different kinds of social work. Take the family caseworker or the youth worker. Both deal with an individual's problems. Other social workers deal with small groups of people. Ada's own specialty is community organization, where she works most comfortably on the policy level, influencing decisions that affect people's lives.

Because her client is the community, Ada does not do much individual counseling. Over the years, most of her energy has been spent in meetings of various committees, commissions, and national boards (and in preparing the paperwork that goes with them). However, because she now teaches a university course (on American Indians), Ada does have the opportunity for individual contact with students.

Just how has Ada Deer made a difference? Having spent her first 18 years on a reservation, Ada is no stranger to Indian life. And it didn't take her long to decide that she would help in the development of her people. Looking back over her activities, both professional and volunteer, she has done just that—from influencing federal legislation aimed at decreasing reservation poverty, to increasing the involvement of American Indians in Girl Scouting. (Ada Deer served as a national board member of Girl Scouts of the U.S.A.)

If you're considering social work as a career, Ada Deer sums up the profession as a "heavy" responsibility that is "exciting, interesting, fulfilling, and at times exhausting and frustrating, too!"

Social Worker

A social worker helps people to resolve personal problems or problems that are aggravated by conditions in society. She/he encourages people to face their difficulties and make progress in resolving them, often with the help of other professionals or social service organizations. The three basic approaches to social work are casework (working on a one-to-one basis), group work (working with groups), or community organization (coordinating the efforts of groups of people to solve community problems). A social worker may also specialize in working with families, the elderly, children, the disadvantaged, or the handicapped.

Special Qualities

mature
sensitive
objective
responsible
able to work independently
concerned about people

Education and Training

A bachelor's degree in social work or a master's degree in social work is required.

Salary Range

$16,700–$45,000

Places of Employment

social service organizations
schools, colleges, and universities
hospitals
clinics

Veterinarian

Well-Being

Dr. Linda Werner is a veterinarian at one of the largest animal hospitals in the country. Quite an impressive position for someone who's only 26 years old.

Linda worked her way up from the bottom, mopping up floors in a kennel. "I was a 'go-for' girl," she recalls. "You know—go for this, go for that. But it was all very worthwhile. It showed me that I could handle blood and feces." The experience also helped get her career off the ground.

Now Linda's duties are a bit more advanced. A typical day? She arrives at work "feeling two hours behind schedule" and spends the morning checking for messages, looking over lab tests, making rounds to examine the animals, and meeting with other doctors to discuss treatments. Then there's time for a sandwich, after which she admits new animals and calms down nervous owners. What makes Linda tick so fast? She explains, "When I see the look on an owner's face, when the owner sees that her dog is healthy again, that's a beautiful feeling."

Linda's work load (about 80 to 90 hours a week) is particularly heavy because she is an intern. Veterinarians in private practice, on the other hand, may set their own pace with allowances for unexpected emergencies. But all veterinarians face the same special problems in their work. Even though animals have personalities just like people, the vet can't always communicate with them. For instance, Linda will often stitch up a dog's wound, only to have the dog chew off the bandage later.

What about being a woman veterinarian? Linda feels one's personality is more important than one's sex, and that if you have the right kind of nature, you'll get along with the animals as well as with their owners!

Veterinarian

A veterinarian cares for animals in the same way a physician cares for human beings. Like the medical doctor, the veterinarian uses surgery, drugs, vaccines, and medical techniques to prevent, diagnose, and treat animal diseases. A veterinarian may specialize in treating small animals and pets, working with farm animals, or inspecting foods and conducting government health programs. All veterinarians, however, safeguard human health by preventing and treating animal diseases, many of which could otherwise be transmitted to people.

Special Qualities

affectionate toward animals
interested in science
observant
studious
inquisitive

Education and Training

A pre-veterinary college program in science or a related field followed by four years at a school of veterinary medicine is necessary.

Salary Range

$20,000–$100,000+

Places of Employment

private practice
animal hospitals
schools of veterinary medicine
laboratories
government agencies

College Professor

People

For Janice Gorn, college teaching was a definite career goal, but she did not reach it early in her life. Previously, Janice worked as a medical technologist, radio announcer, writer, and college administrator. Each job offered new experiences and expanded her knowledge and appreciation of the world around her—its music, art, sciences, and history. Her commitment to sharing her many areas of interest serves her well in her present job as professor of interdisciplinary studies at a large urban university. Janice says teaching gives her the opportunity to "share her passions."

Janice's college teaching career has had many dimensions. She has taught both undergraduate and graduate students, supervised student teachers, and counseled students in both their academic and personal lives. She's especially proud of a program she helped develop to encourage highly qualified older men and women to earn their certification in teaching.

Janice cautions young people aspiring to be professors that colleges and universities are no longer the protected environments they once were where professors could isolate themselves from the problems of society. Today's college professors are expected to plan and teach courses, participate in faculty and community activities, be available to students for independent study and counseling, research and write in their fields of interest, and recruit new students.

Janice finds tremendous rewards in her work. "You get to watch young people grow and open up to ideas even to the point where they are superior to you. Then you know you have really made a contribution to progress," she reports.

College Professor

A college professor presents instruction through lectures, discussions, and/or laboratory work. A professor is expected to do research and write books and articles for publication, and to work with student and community organizations in an advisory or consultative capacity. Over 2,500 colleges and universities in the United States employed about 400,000 full-time and 200,000 part-time faculty in 1974.

Special Qualities

inquisitive
studious
interested in research
able to relate to young adults
able to communicate well
interested in scholarship

Education and Training

A bachelor's degree plus a master's degree or a doctorate in one's special field of interest are almost always required.

Salary Range

$21,300–$40,000+

Places of Employment

colleges and universities
off-campus college centers
correctional institutions
military and industrial training departments

Director of a Multicultural Affairs Organization

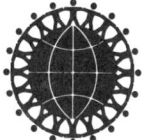

People

As Mary Gaskin, director of a program to expand the awareness of American Indian culture, history, and accomplishments, tells it, "I was sitting and minding my own business when I got a call asking me to take the directorship of the organization. I couldn't say no."

Mary's career has rarely depended so much on chance. As a high school graduate she did what her family and neighbors expected of her—she got a job as a secretary. After time out for marriage and raising her children, she decided to return to work—but not in the secretarial field. With the encouragement of her husband (he took care of the children when she was in class), Mary went back to school and earned her bachelor's and master's degrees and a professional diploma. "Education...I was entranced by it!" she reports.

Today, Mary directs an organization that develops educational programs for and about American Indians. Her satisfaction lies in reaching the students who, prior to these programs, had no way of learning about their rich heritage and culture. Mary explains that she is committed to expanding cultural awareness and respect not only among American Indians but also among other racial and ethnic groups. Mary and her staff try to accomplish these goals through joint meetings as well as educational projects and services to schools, families, and communities.

Even in her "wildest dreams" Mary never thought she'd have a job of this magnitude. No wonder her advice to other teenagers is: "Don't lose sight of your objective and don't let anything stop you." Mary believes that you never need to feel stuck in what you're doing. There's always a way out, and education and training will help lead to a career you really want.

Director of a Multicultural Affairs Organization

Organizations promoting multicultural and multiracial understanding strive to make people aware and appreciative of people from various racial, ethnic, religious, cultural, and social backgrounds. These organizations' goals also include improving the lives of the people they serve educationally, socially, and economically. A director of such an organization works with a staff that includes research specialists, writers, public speakers, program developers, trainers, and reviewers of educational materials. A specialist in this field may also work for an organization which has another major purpose but with a commitment to furthering multicultural and multiracial understanding.

Special Qualities

diplomatic
sensitive to the needs and interests of others
committed to promoting multicultural and multiracial understanding
informed
able to influence and motivate others
able to solve problems
multilingual

Education and Training

A bachelor's degree may or may not be required for most jobs in this field. However, knowledge of sociology, history, and current affairs is helpful. Experience with and exposure to people from a variety of backgrounds is essential.

Salary Range

$10,000–$50,000

Places of Employment

organizations which promote multicultural and multiracial understanding
youth organizations
social service organizations
religious organizations
affirmative action offices
government agencies
industries (personnel departments)
United Nations
television stations
radio stations
educational institutions

Early Childhood Supervisor

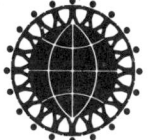

People

"Even though you move up the education career ladder, you are still a teacher," admits early childhood supervisor Ruth Christie with a twinkle in her eye. She's right, too. As you talk to her, Ruth teaches you about the intricacies of her career as a consultant to group day-care programs for children under the age of six.

Ruth began her career in education as a third grade teacher. Then she got an opportunity to work in a day-care center where, she says, "I discovered that children from three to five years of age were my pride and joy." So Ruth went back to college for retraining in early childhood education (her first major had been chemistry), and then on to jobs as assistant teacher, teacher, and finally director of a day-care center. Next, with encouragement from an inspiring colleague, Ruth became an early childhood consultant so that she could be helpful to even more people. "I think it must be thousands of people by now," she reports.

Today, Ruth is a consultant in the day-care division of a city Department of Health which licenses day-care centers. Besides checking health and building facilities, Ruth and her co-workers advise center staff of new educational techniques, useful city services, important legal requirements, and child development concepts. Ruth finds it exciting to be asked questions because she can then share her knowledge and love of children. What are her other rewards? Ruth replies, "A shy child who sits in a corner and then one day begins to relate, or an assistant teacher who announces that she has finally earned her certification to be a fully qualified teacher."

Ruth's goal is to gain the respect and trust of the people with whom she works (boards of directors, center directors, staff, and community). Then she can most freely offer advice gleaned from her rich experience. Ruth believes that for her career "a love of children is important, but not enough. Children need teachers who are firm within limits and have the ability to recognize that each child is different and needs special care and challenges."

Early Childhood Supervisor

An early childhood supervisor administers and coordinates educational programs for children from infancy to age six. She/he observes and works with directors and teachers in nursery schools and day-care centers to make recommendations on educational techniques and to suggest ways to improve educational programs and facilities. Often, an early childhood supervisor offers training through workshops and seminars. Doing research and reading widely to keep up with new developments in the field of interest are also part of a supervisor's job.

Special Qualities

interested in and concerned about young children
able to motivate and support others
skilled in oral and written communication
determined
tactful
multilingual

Education and Training

A bachelor's or master's degree in early childhood education or elementary education is required. Some previous teaching experience at these levels is almost always expected.

Salary Range

$10,000–$35,000

Places of Employment

school districts
nursery schools
day-care centers
college and university experimental schools
government agencies

Economist

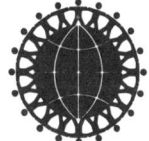

People

What career is in even greater demand when the economy is sluggish and many people are out of work? Would you have thought of economist? Andrea Hahn did, and today she is an analyst at a large economics consulting firm with offices throughout the nation. No wonder economics is the fastest growing college major.

For Andrea, economics offers a disciplined way to solve major problems that affect every citizen's way of life as well as our nation's businesses. Andrea's workday involves conferring with clients and lawyers, analyzing data, reading a lot to keep up with current events and business activity, and writing reports which interpret economic trends and the effect they may have on her clients. To handle the job, Andrea feels you "need to like working with details, but you should also be a generalist, keeping your mind open to all sorts of information. The broader your background and the more interests you have, the better you will be at explaining trends with insight and creativity."

Andrea says she "always expected to work." So, based on her strong math ability and interest in a professional career in the business world, she chose to study economics. When Andrea has to explain an economic trend, she looks at the people behind the numbers, too. She feels economics is special because it encourages her to broaden her interests and puts her in touch with exciting people and ideas.

Andrea loves being a competent professional woman. Although her field is dominated by men, it may not be for long. "Economics offers lots of opportunities for women," says Andrea. For them, it's a "booming" field.

Economist

Economics is concerned with how to utilize resources to provide goods and services for society. An economist studies the problems that arise in the use of such resources as land, raw materials, and manpower. A research economist collects, analyzes, and interprets data on a wide variety of economic issues such as taxation policies, welfare, unemployment, inflation, or recession. She/he then develops theories to explain these conditions, describes different options, and makes recommendations for change.

Special Qualities

able to solve problems
skilled in mathematics
detail-minded
objective
inquisitive
logical
skilled in research and writing

Education and Training

A bachelor's degree is required for entry-level positions. Senior economists must have graduate training in economics or extensive experience in economic analysis.

Salary Range

$22,400–$54,000+

Places of Employment

consulting firms
industries
government agencies and legislative offices
colleges and universities

Fire Dispatcher

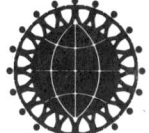

People

How would you like a job where you were responsible for the lives of over one million people? Dorothy Gilliom has such a job—as a fire dispatcher. Although she does admit that her responsibilities put a lot of pressure on her, she's able to act calmly and confidently in every emergency. She's proud, too, of the reputation of the fire department—"fastest response rate in any emergency."

Some people think that the fire department handles only fires, but that isn't really so. From her central relay station, Dorothy receives calls for almost every kind of emergency—from rescuing animals, getting people out of stalled elevators, and delivering babies, to airplane crashes and chemical explosions. She decides how to handle the emergency—by calling out engine-and-ladder companies from all around the city, or by calling on help from other sources (hospitals or the police).

The day Dorothy came to take the test to be a fire dispatcher, the other people in the testing room (all men) told her she was in the wrong place. Dorothy stayed anyway, passed the test with a very high grade, and is now one of only three female fire dispatchers in her city. She likes to encourage more young women and young men to join the force. Dorothy adds, "The uniform fire fighters think it's great when a woman is on the job. They say my voice sounds soothing as well as professional over the radio."

For a job in this demanding field, Dorothy feels you have to be able to put yourself in other people's places in a crisis and be able to help them quickly and calmly. You have to be conscientious and willing to assume a lot of responsibility, too. For Dorothy, the rewards are great. "It's a marvelous feeling to have this job. When I leave work each day, I really know I've accomplished something important."

Fire Dispatcher

A fire dispatcher works at a fire station receiving and communicating information about fires and other emergencies in the community. The dispatcher operates specialized equipment (including computerized machinery) which broadcasts information to other fire stations whose crews, in turn, rush to the scene of the emergency. There are more than 1,000 women currently working as fire dispatchers in fire stations throughout the United States.

Special Qualities
able to use good judgment
able to work on a team
able to work quickly and effectively under pressure
responsible
skilled in oral communication
concerned about people in trouble
detail-minded
multilingual

Education and Training
A high school diploma is usually the minimum educational requirement. Applicants for fire dispatcher jobs must pass written, physical, and medical examinations. Extensive training is given on the job.

Salary Range
$7,500–$20,000

Places of Employment
local fire departments (fire dispatch units)

High School Teacher

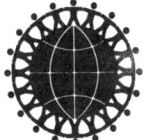

People

Sallie Smith had always been "enamored by history," but it wasn't until her junior year in college that she saw a way to share this love with others. As a young girl she had considered teaching as a career and rejected it. But the inspiration of some of her college professors and the opportunity to participate in a teaching internship at a local high school made her change her mind. She says she "fell in love with teaching" then and there.

Since that time, Sallie has taught history in four high schools in city, suburban, and rural areas. Besides her teaching responsibilities, she has been involved in curriculum development for courses in constitutional law, eastern and western civilization, and problems of democracy. When she is not in the classroom, Sallie can be found meeting with her students for individual counseling or independent study, preparing lectures, or reviewing tests and papers.

Her enthusiasm for the field of education has led her to expand her career role. For example, she has done educational research and evaluation for both a private consulting firm and a large city school district. And she has also trained and supervised student teachers at a local university. In her present position at a private school, Sallie does work in the areas of community relations, alumni affairs, and fund raising. No wonder Sallie says the most frustrating thing about her job is "never having enough time to get everything done!"

But for Sallie, the satisfactions of her job far outweigh its drawbacks. As she says, "Even though I worry that I should do better, I do feel that in some small way I have had a real impact on young people. In her view, teaching is a highly specialized and time-consuming profession which demands sensitivity, flexibility, and intellectual achievement. "You have to be willing to work hard," she acknowledges. And Sallie does!

High School Teacher

A high school teacher (or secondary school teacher) introduces students to a particular subject area. She/he usually conducts five or six classes a day and may have as many as 150 students. A teacher designs classroom presentations to fit a required curriculum, paying careful attention to students' individual needs and abilities. Supervising school clubs, grading papers and tests, working with students on independent projects, and attending meetings with parents and school personnel are also parts of a teacher's job. A teacher's goal is to help students both fulfill their potential and prepare for future roles as citizens, homemakers, and jobholders.

Special Qualities

interested in working with young people
enthusiastic about subject specialty
able to relate to and motivate students
able to communicate well

Education and Training

A bachelor's or master's degree in education or a special subject is necessary. Every state requires high school teachers to be certified to work in public schools.

Salary Range

$10,000–$35,000

Places of Employment

public, parochial, and private high schools and boarding schools
correctional facilities

Historian

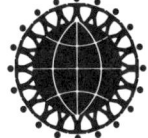

People

Betty Lee Sung, historian and ethnic studies researcher, explains her career this way: "Sometimes the job you want just doesn't exist, so you go out and make yourself a job." And that's just what she did.

It all started when Betty worked as a radio scriptwriter for a program about Chinese Americans. She found that researching her scripts was difficult because so little had been written on the topic. As Betty says, "More and more Chinese Americans were coming to the United States, but we didn't know where we were going or where we had been." So, even though she had a large family to care for, Betty saw she had a new mission. She began to fulfill it by writing one of the first and finest books about Chinese Americans in the United States, and she hasn't stopped her studies since.

With the publication of her book, Betty became recognized as an expert in her field and was asked to teach one of the first courses in Asian American studies at a large city college. Betty believes that ethnic studies provides a good opportunity for people to appreciate different ethnic groups and to understand how social, political, and economic influences affect different groups. Betty acknowledges, "I'm a historian of the present as much as the past." Her understanding of people's feelings and values helps her in suggesting solutions to present-day problems like housing and unemployment.

"The most fascinating thing about teaching is dealing with young minds," she observes. "I have gotten fantastic solutions to problems I have posed to my students." Even though there are more publications about Chinese Americans available now than when Betty wrote her book, she still must do research in the community to keep in touch with current ideas and attitudes. Betty loves the challenge and creativity the job allows her and is glad for the support of her students. But she still admits, "Being a pioneer isn't easy."

Historian

History is the record of events, institutions, ideas, and people. A historian describes and analyzes the past through writing, teaching, and research. Then she/he relates this understanding of the past to current events in an effort to explain the present. Specialties in this field include history of a specific country, area, or period of time, and history of a particular field such as economics, military affairs, the labor movement, art, or architecture. Most historians are also college and university professors who lecture as well as write and do research.

Special Qualities

interested in reading and research
skilled in oral and written communication
curious
detail-minded
able to understand trends and relationships

Education and Training

A bachelor's degree is sufficient for some beginning jobs, but a master's degree or doctorate is preferred (even essential) for high-level teaching, research, and administrative positions.

Salary Range

$14,800–$51,000

Places of Employment

high schools, colleges, and universities
research institutes
museums
libraries
government agencies
historical societies

Human Resources Administrator

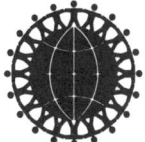

People

As someone who once dreamed of being a surgeon, and today as the supervisor of 3,000 people responsible for a major city's family and adult services, Gladys Harrington admits, "I guess I have always been attracted to crisis-oriented jobs." With responsibilities for 178 separate programs, Gladys has found the right place to use her many talents.

It was as a college student that Gladys discovered she "had a knack for organizing people." During those years she worked in the civil rights movement and as a community activist. Although Gladys also has experience as a social caseworker, her academic background is in business and management. In her present position as deputy administrator of a city human resources administration, she puts both her experience and formal training to work in the human services area.

Gladys has a real commitment to working within government to accomplish needed social goals. "I didn't see any hope for making changes unless I could work within the structure," she says. Gladys spends her workdays meeting with state and local officials, planning programs with agency heads, discussing the legal aspects of the work of her department, persuading city legislators to approve her programs, and talking "incessantly" on the telephone. What does Gladys do when things get too hectic? She visits one of the programs she is responsible for to see firsthand how her work is really helping. Then, refreshed, she returns to her nonstop pace. Gladys feels that the pressure of her job is legitimate because she "works for the taxpayers." She claims her biggest frustration is not having the time to accomplish all she would like to do.

Gladys would like to see more women come into government—especially if they bring an interest in management along with special skills and knowledge in such areas as social services, day care, housing, or environment. She believes that "when women come into government agencies, they bring extra sensitivity to their work."

Human Resources Administrator

A human resources administrator (also called a social service administrator or public administrator) plans, supervises, and implements programs to help the disadvantaged, the elderly, and families and individuals in distress. Working within government or private agencies, the human resources administrator proposes new service programs and, at the same time, tries to improve existing services and to alleviate the need for crisis-oriented services so that more energy can be directed toward positive, preventive social support programs. Often, high-level administrators take on a great deal of financial responsibility as part of their job.

Special Qualities

concerned about people and social problems
business-minded
able to motivate, direct, and support others
multilingual

Education and Training

A bachelor's degree with a major in social work, sociology, psychology, public administration, or business administration is required. Often, a master's degree or a doctorate is required for the highest level positions.

Salary Range

$12,540–$38,500

Places of Employment

government agencies
social service organizations
hospitals

Information Officer in the Armed Forces

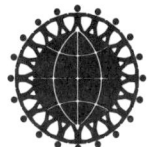

People

Driving home from work one day, Juliann Lepore took a detour—to the Armed Forces recruiting office to enlist. Although this news was somewhat of a surprise to Juliann's family, it didn't surprise Juliann. As she says, "I knew I wanted a career with a purpose. I had researched opportunities in the Armed Forces, and when I learned that the branch I was most interested in promoted women equally with men, I was ready to go." That very day she did go—to her first assignment halfway across the country.

Since then, Captain Lepore has been stationed in many places in the United States and abroad. Combining her interests with the available opportunities in her branch of the service has meant jobs in intelligence, as a command officer at a base, and now as an information officer at the Pentagon in Washington. Her career has been a smorgasbord of challenges and options—from teaching people what plants to eat when they need to live off the land, to aircraft recognition, to responding to newspaper reporters' requests for information on congressional travel to military bases.

She finds the same advantages to this career now that she saw in the very beginning when she enlisted. She gets more and more education and experience and earns a salary at the same time. Most of all, Juliann likes her job because she is moving all the time. "I get it all together and am never bored. I work on all sorts of topics and assignments."

Juliann thinks this is a great time to join the Armed Forces. Opportunities for women, both single and married, are increasing. What should you bring to this career to find satisfaction? Juliann answers with assurance, "A feeling for your country and the readiness to go with every new assignment."

Careers in the Armed Forces

The Armed Forces—Army, Air Force, Navy, Marine Corps, and Coast Guard—employ over two million individuals in a range of occupations almost as wide as those found in civilian life. It is possible to pursue hundreds of career interests from clerical work to a medical specialty to construction. Young adults may enlist in any one of a variety of programs that involves a combination of active and reserve duty. Three- and four-year enlistments are most common. Military personnel are stationed throughout the United States and in many foreign countries.

Special Qualities

Special qualities depend upon the type of career interest one chooses to pursue. Today, women are eligible and encouraged to enter almost all military occupational fields.

Education and Training

Although a high school diploma is desired, it is not necessary for enlistment in the Armed Forces. However, certain specialties may require additional education. To enter as an officer, one needs a bachelor's degree. All the Armed Forces offer extensive on-duty training and educational opportunities to help candidates qualify for advancement and pursue their personal interests.

Salary Range

$10,000–$40,000
(Includes room and board, medical and dental care, shopping privileges, a military clothing allowance, and vacation and travel opportunities.)

Places of Employment

military bases and civilian locations all over the world

U.S. Department of Defense

International Program Officer

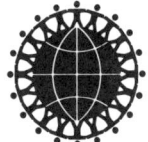

People

In the quiet of her office, Adrienne Germain does not appear to have the problems of women around the world on her mind. But she does. Each year, Adrienne, an international program officer, travels to Asia, Africa, Latin America, the Caribbean, and the Middle East to speak with women about their concerns as their countries become industrialized and modernized. For a woman who wanted a career that was intellectually stimulating and would contribute to the progress of human welfare, Adrienne has found more than enough of a challenge.

Adrienne's first job involved researching the effects of population growth throughout the world. As her career developed, her concern for women became broader. Today, when the philanthropic foundation for which she works gives a grant to a developing country, Adrienne studies how these funded programs will change women's lives economically, socially, and within their families. Whether she is in Indonesia studying new methods of rice harvesting, or in Latin America evaluating a new economic policy, Adrienne asks herself, "What effect will these developments have on the women here?" Adrienne often discovers that improvements may have negative effects, too. Her job is to improve understanding of the problems as well as the benefits of progress, and to suggest ways to make progress work for all.

The most exciting part of the job for Adrienne is the contact with people, especially "the extraordinary women," who are making an important impact on the lives of others. "We are guests in each country," she acknowledges, "but we like to think that our efforts will contribute to policy making in countries in which we share a commitment to important social and economic goals."

If young women are fascinated by other cultures, can learn foreign languages, like to travel, and have a strong interest in the social sciences, Adrienne would encourage them to join her in this career.

International Program Officer

An international program officer plans and monitors programs and activities supported by her/his organization in countries throughout the world. These programs may be agricultural, economic, social, or cultural. The program officer is invited by a participating country to observe the progress of projects, and to develop ways together to improve and share successful practices. International relations work often involves extensive foreign travel to meet with the people involved in a particular project, followed by detailed oral and written reports.

Special Qualities

concerned about people of different cultures
adaptable
multilingual
skilled in oral and written communication
interested in foreign affairs
able to work well with others
self-motivated

Education and Training

A bachelor's degree in the social sciences (history, political science, economics) is generally required for entry positions. For higher level positions, a master's degree or doctorate is preferred. Knowledge of foreign languages and experience living abroad are added assets.

Salary Range

$10,000–$50,000

Places of Employment

foundations
research institutes
United Nations
government agencies

Lawyer

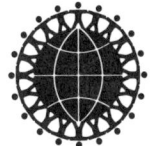

People

When Nancy Young went to law school, she attended with 12 other women and 525 men. Now things have changed as more and more women are pursuing careers in law. But Nancy is still doing exceptional things—she has her own firm and she works in all areas of law, a career style that has become less common as many lawyers now join large firms which specialize in certain types of legal work. "I always wanted to be in private practice," she admits from her offices at home where she must constantly keep up with her many clients (75 or more at a time).

Nancy takes all kinds of cases—criminal, business, family, and real estate, to name only a few. On a typical day, she might be in court in the morning and in her office in the afternoon interviewing clients, dictating lengthy letters and reports, researching, and doing telephone work. Although Nancy works at an exhausting pace under a lot of pressure and tight deadlines, she probably wouldn't have it any other way. For her, the satisfactions far outweigh the frustrations. "You have the feeling that through your efforts you have directly helped another human being, and that with your energy, effort, and professional background you can really make a positive difference. There is nothing more rewarding than that." Now that Nancy has her own successful firm, she's not about to sit back and relax. Future plans for her include expanding her firm and doing more volunteer legal work in the community.

Nancy recommends that a young woman considering law ask herself if she is logical, articulate, and resilient. "You have to be able to reason, and to think, write, and speak clearly and logically," says Nancy. It's equally important that you have a tremendous capacity to absorb pressures from other people and can maintain a professional approach, putting your own problems aside and concentrating on the problems of others. Nancy worked hard to achieve her goals. As she says, "I'm one of the fortunate people. I love what I do."

Lawyer

A lawyer (or attorney) advises her/his clients about their rights and responsibilities in a variety of areas including buying and selling property, making wills, and conducting business. A lawyer also negotiates the settlement of legal problems out of court or, when necessary, represents clients in court or before government agencies. It is becoming more common, especially in large cities, for lawyers to specialize in one branch of law such as corporate, criminal, labor, patent, real estate, tax, or international law.

Special Qualities

able to argue persuasively
interested in working with people and ideas
logical
detail-minded
skilled in oral and written communication
interested in research
able to apply knowledge of the past to current situations

Education and Training

A bachelor's degree and a graduate law degree are usually required. A candidate must also pass the state Bar Association qualifying examination.

Salary Range

$22,500–$100,000+

Places of Employment

law firms
businesses and corporations
government agencies
city, state, and federal legislatures
self-employment

Political Scientist

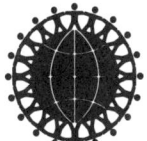

People

How would you like to come home from work every day "feeling great?" Philippa Strum does. Philippa is a political scientist, author, professor, and mother of three young children. How does she do it all? As she says, "The responsibilities of my work and the responsibilities of motherhood balance each other very well. One role helps to relieve the tensions of another role."

Philippa spends three days a week teaching courses in American government to undergraduates at a local college. Two days a week she retreats to her study or the library to do the research and reading which keeps her up-to-date in her field and helps her prepare her articles and books for publication. Because she is able to schedule her out-of-class time to fit her home as well as her professional responsibilities, Philippa can give her family the time and attention they need.

Philippa does more than teach facts to her students. "I help students recognize the relationship of the world to their own lives. They grow in intellectual problem solving and become better citizens." Philippa is proud of the fact that her students know about her family responsibilities. "I function as a model. I help young women to see that they can combine a family with a demanding career like that of a political scientist." Research gives an added dimension to Philippa's life. "It is fascinating to work in the world of ideas and to study why people think and act as they do."

Philippa sees women students' growing interest in political science as a hopeful sign for more women entering her profession. In the future, Philippa believes more women will be asking themselves if they have the organizational ability and stamina to work in this field. Where there are women like Philippa, who could doubt that it's possible!

Political Scientist

A political scientist studies governments—their structures, purposes, and methods. She/he can specialize in a general area of political science (political theory, United States political institutions and processes, comparative government), in a particular type of political organization, or in the politics of a particular time in history. Most political scientists are college and university professors. They combine research, consultation, and administrative duties with teaching. Some political scientists are primarily researchers. Others analyze the operations of government agencies or administer government programs.

Special Qualities
interested in current events
detail-minded
interested in reading and research
skilled in oral and written communication
objective
able to work independently and with others

Education and Training
A bachelor's degree in political science, government, or international relations is required. For high-level positions, a master's degree or doctorate is required.

Salary Range
$21,000–$50,000

Places of Employment
colleges and universities
research institutes
foundations
government agencies
opinion research organizations

Post Office Supervisor

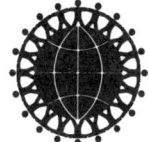

People

For a woman who says she "really wanted to advance," Eunice Ellis's career history certainly shows a desire fulfilled. Each time an opportunity for promotion was available at the post office where she works, Eunice applied for and earned a more responsible job. Today she has a supervisory position—general foreman, mails.

Eunice works the evening tour of duty (7:00 P.M. to 3:30 A.M.) at a terminal post office. She schedules and assigns her staff to the tasks of sorting and processing the millions of pieces of mail that come in each day. She also analyzes reports, keeps records, and evaluates staff performance. When problems come up, Eunice is there to help work them out so that the mails go through. Her job is more than just processing mail. Says Eunice, "I deal with the people." And that's what makes every government service work.

Eunice's evening and weekend work schedule enabled her to complete her bachelor's and master's degrees. Now she is thinking of studying for a doctorate in public administration. When asked how her two teenagers feel about her determination in her career and academic life, Eunice smiles and says, "Ever since they've known me, I've been working. They just accept it."

To insure that women have upward mobility into highly responsible positions, the U.S. Postal Service has recently initiated a program to recruit and advance capable women. This development, coupled with Eunice's own success story, should inspire other women to consider careers in this branch of the government. Eunice advises, "Get as much education as you can and apply for every vacancy you are interested in. Women have a promising future here."

Post Office Supervisor

The United States Postal Service employs about 700,000 workers to process and deliver mail. The postmaster and supervisors are responsible for the day-to-day operations of the post office, for hiring and promoting employees, and for setting up work schedules. Other postal service careers include postal clerks, city and rural mail carriers, mail handlers, maintenance workers, motor vehicle operators, and postal inspectors.

Special Qualities

conscientious
hard-working
able to supervise and motivate others
accurate

Education and Training

An applicant for a postal service job must pass an examination and meet the minimum age requirement. Many postal service jobs do not require formal education. On-the-job training is offered.

Salary Range

$13,000–$30,000

Places of Employment

United States post offices and postal service offices
businesses and corporations (mailroom departments)

Program Services Director

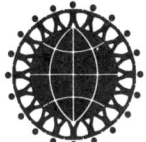

People

What do you do when you have training in a variety of fields? Do you choose just one for a career? Not if you're Maria "Cecilia" Cordeiro. She has a job that combines all her skills—that of program services director for a local Girl Scout council. That way, everybody—from Brownies up—gets to benefit from her experiences.

For Cecilia, early training in elementary education, working with families, and teaching the blind were separate activities in her native Brazil. But her leisure time activities (working with a Boy Scout pack) provided a common thread. (In fact, it was the experience that made her change her childhood career choice from lawyer to teacher.) Cecilia learned through her Boy Scout experience that she liked camping and working with children in real-life learning situations. She also grew to like her co-leader, and eventually married him. As Cecilia says, "My life has taken many turns due to my interest in the scouting movement."

Today, Cecilia has responsibility for developing and implementing Girl Scout program for 15,000 girls in a large suburban Girl Scout council. Some days this means planning the details of council-sponsored events. Other days find Cecilia putting together written materials to be used by girls in group programs.

Cecilia's lifestyle and her family responsibilities have played an important part in deciding her career direction. When she first approached her local council, there were too many adult volunteers (can you imagine that!). Cecilia had to wait until her daughter was Brownie-age to find a volunteer spot. But once involved, Cecilia never stopped moving—from leader, to trainer, to field executive, to camp director, to her current position. And all along the way, from her days in college to her Girl Scouting position, she has met women she admired who "helped pull me along and made me grow."

Where will Cecilia "grow" next? A recent degree in accounting has opened up the business world to Cecilia and she hopes to find a way to combine it with her job to increase both her responsibilities and her income. As she says, "My kids will be ready for college soon." Knowing what that means—in dollars and cents—helps Cecilia look forward to new challenges.

Copyright ©1978 Girl Scouts of the United States of America

Program Services Director

A program services director plans and implements programs for girls ages 6 to 17 in local Girl Scout councils. She/he identifies program needs, does research, writes materials, and participates in workshops designed to train leaders in the use of materials. The program services director may also plan and conduct events for girls.

Special Qualities
interested in development of girls and young women
skilled in oral and written communication
curious
inventive
able to organize events and people
able to get along well with people from diverse backgrounds

Education and Training
A college degree in education, recreation, or youth work is desirable. Experience and interest in working with youth in an informal setting is an asset.

Salary Range
$18,000–$106,000

Places of Employment
Girl Scout councils
youth organizations
community centers

School Administrator

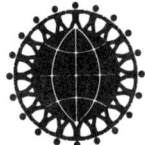

People

Most school administrators are principals who supervise schools of their own. But Eda Lepelstat is a school administrator with a difference. She is a central office administrator who coordinates programs in a large city school system for thousands of children who are physically handicapped and have learning disabilities.

Eda began her career as a special education teacher working with brain injured, physically handicapped, and emotionally disturbed children. Her teaching ability and experience working in experimental programs provided a firm foundation for her current position. Today, as central office administrator, Eda keeps track of all the teachers and students in classes for the physically handicapped. But that's not all. The most important part of her job is to develop new programs for children. Meeting with parents and teachers, writing project plans and budgets, and obtaining funds for new programs are all part of a day's work for Eda.

Even though Eda is often frustrated by lack of money to do all the things she'd like to see done, the satisfactions of her job are great. "I see children who have been left out, who have suffered years of school failure. Then they enter a new program and grow. Even though they don't know me, I know I have played an important part in their success."

Although women are commonly found as classroom teachers, there are also opportunities for women in school administration. If you're willing to take on a lot of responsibility and work under pressure, there are places for you in this field.

School Administrator

A school administrator works with the teaching staff and, in some cases, the community school board, to develop educational policies and to plan and supervise the curriculum. She/he may also be responsible for the school's budget, personnel, equipment, building maintenance, and services. Job titles which involve aspects of school administration include principal, headmaster, headmistress, superintendent, project director, and dean of students.

Special Qualities
able to lead others
detail-minded
determined
self-motivated
interested in community service
able to communicate

Education and Training
A bachelor's or master's degree in education and some teaching experience are required. Many states require that administrators working in public schools be licensed.

Salary Range
$15,000–$65,000

Places of Employment
public, private, and parochial schools
central school offices

Sociologist

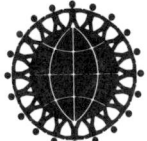

People

People-watching can be a lot of fun. But did you know that it could also be a career? For Ann Pasanella, research sociologist, people-watching has become a rewarding and absorbing way of life.

Ann works at a large university-affiliated research institute. As she says, "I look for patterns in human behavior." Sociologists believe that people tend to do things because of the groups and the social backgrounds they come from. Sociologists ask questions about how people learn these social behaviors, and how the unwritten rules of group behavior affect people's lives.

As a director of a number of projects conducted by her institute, Ann plans ways to study these questions. Her projects may involve questionnaires to probe the thoughts of many different people on a topic, or case studies where all the individuals in a particular group are interviewed to determine their ideas about an organization or about what it means to be a part of their group. But knowing what people think and how groups act isn't enough. Sociological research is also dedicated to making recommendations that are used by government, social agencies, and businesses. "We are rewarded when we have thought of new ways to attack social problems, and when we have given others stepping stones in understanding what people are all about," Ann says proudly.

Ann feels that advanced education beyond college is essential for a career in sociology. "You will be working on your own—reading, researching, and doing lots of writing. You need to like being a student because the more knowledge you have, the more insights you will be able to bring to your work." Ann believes commitment, strong skills, and support from your professors are very important when looking for a place in this field.

Sociologist

A sociologist studies how people behave in groups such as families, tribes, communities, religious sects, political parties, and business organizations. Using tests, surveys, and experiments, a sociologist studies the origin and growth of a group, the effect of group activities on individual members, and the behaviors and interaction of groups. Specialties in this field include intergroup relations, family problems, population studies, criminology, community planning, and public relations in industry. Most sociologists are college and university professors, but the number of those who work as researchers, consultants, and administrators outside academic institutions is increasing.

Special Qualities

interested in study and research
skilled in oral and written communication
able to work independently and with others
curious about human behavior
objective

Education and Training

A bachelor's degree in sociology is almost always required. For higher level positions, a master's degree or a doctorate is preferred.

Salary Range

$14,800–$50,000

Places of Employment

research institutes
colleges and universities
government agencies
businesses
opinion research organizations

Accountant

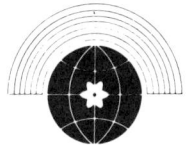

Today and Tomorrow

Like thousands of other girls, when Florence Corsello was growing up, she boosted her allowance by baby-sitting on weekends. But unlike most, Florence kept precise records of the money she earned and spent. At the time, however, Florence had no idea she was calculating a career in accounting.

As a senior accountant in a public accounting firm, Florence works with clients checking financial statements and records for accuracy. But if you picture her sitting behind a desk hunched over a column of numbers, guess again. As Florence says, "This job is more than math. If I'm sitting behind my desk all day, I'm not doing my job." She explains that for every dollar figure on a financial statement, she must dig up supporting evidence which can't be found on her desk. She recalls one client in a 34-story building. "I spent half the day in the elevator going from one floor to the next."

Depending on the company's size, an audit can take anywhere from one week to one year. After all the telephoning, letter writing, record reading, and inventory taking that may be necessary for an audit, Florence feels particularly good when she finally issues the statement about the company's finances.

But there may be obstacles along the way. For example, because Florence must go to her client's office to conduct the audit, she is often seen as an outsider. Getting cooperation means breaking down that barrier. "You have to be a bit of a diplomat," she confides.

Any other advice for an aspiring accountant? If you're persistent and thorough, and strive for accuracy and can communicate with people, you're off to a good start. According to Florence, the opportunities exist, but "you must pursue them with dedication."

Accountant

An accountant prepares and analyzes financial reports. Many accountants specialize in doing audits (reviewing a financial statement and judging its reliability). Others may prepare income tax forms or advise individual clients and major businesses about budgeting, taxes, and investments.

Special Qualities
skilled in mathematics
neat
accurate
able to work independently
responsible

Education and Training
A bachelor's degree in accounting or a closely related major is usually needed. (Educational requirements in this field may vary depending on the employer.)

Salary Range
$20,500–$80,000+

Places of Employment
accounting firms
government agencies
businesses and industries
colleges and universities
self-employment

Anthropologist

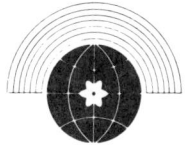

Today and Tomorrow

The mystery of museums, especially natural history museums, captured Flora Kaplan's imagination when she was young. As she recalls, "The figures seemed so lifelike; the jewelry and the costumes so real." Then, in high school, Flora's fascination became the theme of her first published story in which she imagined herself locked in a museum overnight. Little did she know at the time that her childhood fantasy would soon become reality.

As an anthropologist, Flora began studying civilizations of the past as an assistant curator in a primitive art museum. Her work involved research, some label writing, and typing. According to Flora, "I was chief cook and bottle washer." But at long last, she was behind the scenes, in and out of storerooms—touching, studying, and caring for relics. Then came the appointment to acting curator, followed by time out for two children and a Ph.D. degree.

Today, Dr. Kaplan is an assistant professor of anthropology at a major university. Her teaching responsibilities include ongoing research and regularly scheduled courses.

What Flora appreciates most about anthropology is that it's never boring. Whether you're studying past civilizations or living cultural groups, when your subject is people, "everything is grist for your mill"—even bathroom graffiti, the theme of her latest research project. But an anthropologist is also sensitive to moral and ethical dilemmas. As she explains, "When you study people, you come to care about them. You learn about problems such as widespread poverty, but often you're powerless to help."

What can Flora tell a young girl who's curious about this field? "If you're interested in anthropology, follow your inclination. It will enrich your life in a million ways."

Anthropologist

An anthropologist studies people—their origins, physical characteristics, and cultures. There are four areas of specialization: studying cultures to learn about different ways of life, studying the remains of past civilizations, studying languages, or studying how man's physical characteristics have evolved over the centuries. Most anthropologists combine college or university teaching with research.

Special Qualities
interested in natural history
interested in reading and research
able to write well
able to work independently
willing to travel

Education and Training
A bachelor's degree in anthropology is required. Generally, a master's degree is needed for higher level positions.

Salary Range
$14,800–$40,000

Places of Employment
colleges and universities
museums
government agencies

Astronaut

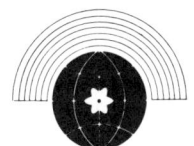

Today and Tomorrow

When it came time for Rhea Seddon to choose a career, the sky was not the limit. Rhea, who describes herself as a "typical tomboy from the south" recalls thinking when the first men landed on the moon, "That's something I'd really like to do!" At the time, Rhea summed up her chances as "far-fetched" (there were no female astronauts); but just in case, she decided to play it smart.

Knowing that a science background is a must for any astronaut, Rhea prepared for a career in medicine (surgery), taking time out when she could to earn her private pilot's license. "If there was something I could do to improve my odds, I did it," she recalls. Rhea must have done something right. After applications, interviews, and tests (both physical and psychological), she was one of 35 selected for the space program out of a total of 8,100 applicants!

As a mission specialist astronaut, Dr. Seddon will conduct scientific experiments aboard a spacecraft orbiting anywhere from 7 to 30 days. But before that, she must spend two years training for this special mission when she will learn all aspects of the space flight—from computers and communication systems to actually piloting the shuttle. And once she has all this information down pat, she'll spend week after week putting this knowledge into practice on simulated flights and weightless walks. Needless to say, Rhea is excited about being involved in the space program. "It's like being part of a Columbus voyage!"

What can she tell an aspiring young astronaut? Rhea, who first became a doctor instead of an astronaut and is now an astronaut instead of a doctor, offers some down-to-earth advice. "Develop your science background and plan an alternative career because this one is highly competitive." But more important, Rhea adds, "Dare to take a chance. If I didn't, I wouldn't be here today!"

Astronaut

There are two types of astronauts: pilots and mission specialists. Pilots navigate the spacecraft. Mission specialists coordinate shuttle operations. Basically, the mission specialist plans crew activities and the use of food and other necessities, and conducts experiments in the payload (work area) of the spacecraft. She/he must have a detailed understanding of the shuttle system, the requirements and objectives of the mission, and the equipment for each experiment on the mission.

Special Qualities

physically fit
skilled and interested in science
able to solve mechanical problems
emotionally stable
persistent
adventurous
able to handle emergency situations

Education and Training

For a pilot, an advanced college degree in engineering, physical science, or math, and at least 1,000 hours of pilot time with experience in high performance jet aircraft or flight testing are required. For a mission specialist, an advanced college degree in engineering, physical science, math, or biological sciences is required. It is not necessary to be an aircraft pilot. Both pilots and mission specialists must complete a two-year training program.

Salary Range

$15,000–$40,000

Places of Employment

space centers

Auto Mechanic

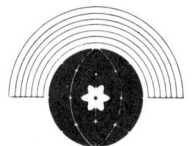

Today and Tomorrow

Donna Huber always dreamed of becoming a race car driver. Though today she may not be racing cars professionally, her present job isn't far off the track.

As a mechanic at a major automotive service center, Donna spends her day working in the battery department. After changing into her uniform (in the ladies' room; there's no women's locker room yet), she greets a steady flow of customers (usually around 30 and more in cold weather). First, she checks out the charging system, including battery, alternator, regulator, and starter. Then, when she has identified the problem, the repairs begin. Although she most often installs new batteries, other repairs can range from readjusting belts to replacing alternators.

No matter what the repair, however, the best part of the job for Donna is getting to the source of the problem. "Finding out what's wrong makes me feel good," she notes. On the other hand, job pressure builds when customers complain of long lines. And Donna finds it particularly annoying when an occasional customer (man or woman) refuses to let her work on the car because she's female. "I was really hurt," she says about her feelings the first time it happened. Perhaps this incident explains why Donna tries to do just a little better than her male co-workers.

What about the immediate future? Donna hopes to move out of the battery department into front ends (ball joints and wheel alignments) where there's more challenge. When asked where she'll be ten years from now, she smiles and says, "You know, I still have this thing for racing."

Auto Mechanic

An auto mechanic diagnoses car breakdowns and makes the necessary repairs. After hearing the owner's description of the problem, the mechanic may use testing equipment to identify its source, and then will make the necessary adjustment, replacement, or repair. An auto mechanic also checks cars periodically to be sure they are safe and trouble free.

Special Qualities
knowledgeable about automobiles
able to analyze automotive problems
mechanically minded

Education and Training
On-the-job training and/or training at a vocational school are ways to prepare for this career.

Salary Range
$12,600–$40,000

Places of Employment
automobile dealers
automobile repair shops
gasoline service stations

Carpenter

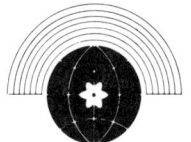

Today and Tomorrow

Mary Garvin always wanted to be an artist. (She has a college degree in fine arts to prove it.) Today, Mary may not be using paint brushes and palette knives, but her artwork does require tools of another trade.

"They started me off with a 90-pound jackhammer!" says Mary, a five-foot-six, 125-pound construction worker, about the time she was hired to work on a high-rise building project. But once her supervisor saw she could "tow the line," Mary was taken off jackhammers and told to get down to brass tacks. As a carpenter, Mary typically uses her skills to build stairs, rails, concrete forms, catwalks, and carports.

What's in it for Mary? A lot. She explains that the money is good and carpentry is a healthy, "puritan" job. "There's never any question that you've earned a day's pay." Sure, she's tired at the end of the day. But she adds, "That's a good feeling." And between projects she has time off for her artwork.

Although Mary likes what she does, the pace at which she works isn't always agreeable. "I don't like being rushed." She recalls the times she hadn't even finished building a form and the trucks were already pouring concrete around her feet. (Mary bought high boots for this purpose alone.)

What about a woman on a construction crew? According to Mary, you don't have to be big and strong. As she says, "Not all construction workers are six-foot-five. All you have to know is that you *can* do it. After that, it's easy."

Carpenter

A carpenter constructs and repairs building structures. Her/his assignment may be to construct frameworks for buildings; to build doors, cabinets, and stairs; to install windows and wall paneling; to lay hardwood floors; or to build the forms into which concrete is poured.

Special Qualities

able to work well with hands
able to work on high structures without fear of falling
has a good sense of balance
physically fit
able to understand basic mathematics
able to get along with others

Education and Training

An apprenticeship program which usually includes four years of on-the-job training and some classroom work is required.

Salary Range

$12,000–$45,000

Places of Employment

construction companies
manufacturing firms
government agencies
utilities companies
self-employment

Computer Operator

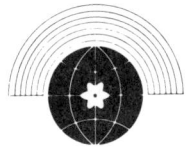

Today and Tomorrow

You walk down a long corridor to a door marked Data Processing and show the guard your private pass. The sliding doors close behind you. Inside, you're greeted by flashing lights, typewriters typing without typists, and the steady hum of machinery. At first glance, this setting seems very official, if somewhat overwhelming. Official? Absolutely! Overwhelming? Look closer....

"There's nothing to it," says Mildred McMullen about her job as a computer operator. "It's easier than you think." Basically, Mildred's work involves loading computers with keypunched cards or magnetic tapes. Then, once the computer is started, she watches the machine closely, looking for error lights that signal a problem. If the computer stops or the Halt button lights up, Mildred has to find out where the snag is.

In the course of a day, Mildred runs about 12 jobs, each lasting about 20 minutes. Mildred is happy to report that major breakdowns don't happen often. But what about the little mechanical mistakes such as paper jams? "That's frustrating," says Mildred, "but it's a fact of life." On an average, she'll send for a computer repair person three or four times a week.

In a job that seems so mechanical, Mildred has no problem managing a smile, or correcting mistakes, either. She explains that in the computer field, you can't be afraid to try something new or make an occasional mistake. She adds that although errors happen, "it's not the end of the world." For Mildred, however, a job as computer operator is no mistake. In her words, "I wouldn't trade this job for anything."

Computer Operator

The computer operator processes the program (data on punch cards or magnetic tapes) that has been prepared by the computer programmer. After correct cards or tapes are loaded, the computer operator starts the machine. She watches the computer carefully and, if an error light flashes or the computer stops, the operator must get to the source of the problem and start the machine once again.

Special Qualities
analytical
able to reason well
able to use good judgment
interested in working with machines
patient

Education and Training
A high school diploma and some additional training in computer operating are preferred.

Salary Range
$12,800–$29,000

Places of Employment
manufacturing firms
data processing services
banks
insurance companies
government agencies

Computer Programmer

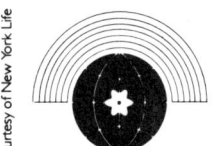

Today and Tomorrow

Shirley Bolden was always fascinated with linguistics. In fact, she had her sights set on translating as a career choice. Her job in a large insurance company isn't exactly what she had in mind at the time, but it does involve linguistics of another sort.

"I speak the language of computers," Shirley says about her job. Contrary to popular opinion, Shirley claims that computers don't think for themselves and, furthermore, they don't understand English. In order to do a job, they must have instructions in an understandable language. That's where Shirley comes in.

Shirley plans instructions, or programs, for these computers. Once the plan is set, she translates her ideas into a code that computers can follow. If, for example, the assignment is to print all the customer bills scheduled to be mailed on October 25, Shirley programs the computer to search the company's 6,000,000 policy-holder records, selecting and printing bills only for that date. Within two hours, the computer has the bills (50,000 on a typical day) printed and ready to mail.

Shirley really likes the problem-solving part of programming. Even when there's a bug (error) in the plan, she sees it as a personal challenge. It's computer breakdowns, however, that she finds most aggravating. Also, because computers are continually updated, just as Shirley becomes familiar with one, another takes its place. That can be frustrating. But the job has advantages too, like traveling out of town to go to computer learning centers or conferences.

Shirley, who had her heart set on one particular computer job, was turned down the first time around. But she's equally happy about her present job. As she says, "Don't ever stop trying. If you're set on one job and it doesn't pan out, try another!"

77

Computer Programmer

A computer programmer writes detailed instructions, or programs, for computers. A program lists in logical order the steps the machine must follow to solve a problem. For example, in order to bill customers, the computer must be programmed to find the old balance, add the new charges, and deduct payments. Programs may deal with scientific as well as business problems, and a programmer usually specializes in one or the other.

Special Qualities

logical
analytical
patient
persistent
accurate
ingenious

Education and Training

Training requirements vary. Depending on the employer, any of the following may be required: a bachelor's degree with no special major, a bachelor's degree with a science major, or training at a technical school.

Salary Range

$14,800–$43,100+

Places of Employment

manufacturing firms
data processing services
banks
insurance companies
government agencies

Drafter

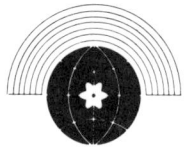

Today and Tomorrow

Lydia Gorecki says it took more than training to take her career plans off the drawing board and make them come alive. Lydia is an architectural drafter. In addition to a steady hand, "you have to be neat, organized, and very precise," she says about lettering and line drawing—her day-to-day drafting activities.

Because builders work directly from her plans, she also has to be meticulous. If, for example, Lydia is drafting plans to renovate one floor of a building including heating, lighting, and ventilation systems, she begins by studying the engineers' sketches. Next, she uses her tools (T-square, rulers, pencils, and plenty of erasers) to translate the engineers' ideas into detailed drawings—from pipes to partitions, complete with dimensions and specifications. Occasionally, she visits field sites with an engineer to take measurements and survey electrical outlets. And, as a welcome change of pace, Lydia prepares charts and graphs for company conferences.

Although Lydia enjoys her job, she can't picture herself drafting forever. She has a college degree in interior design, so it's understandable that she's looking to move into a job that involves a little more designing and a little less drawing.

How can you tell if a drafting career is designed for you? Lydia, a good ex-doodler, admits that doodles really don't have much to do with drafting. But she adds, "Look at your lettering. If it's neat, even, and readable, your blueprints will be too!"

Drafter

To build a bridge, a building, or even to renovate a room, to manufacture a radio, a satellite, or a child's toy, workers must follow a plan which gives the exact dimensions and specifications of the entire object and each of its parts. A drafter prepares these detailed plans, based on sketches and calculations of engineers, architects, and designers. A drafter may specialize in various fields including mechanical, electrical, electronic, aeronautical, structural, or architectural drafting. Tools of the trade include compasses, dividers, protractors, triangles, and machines that combine the functions of several of these devices.

Special Qualities
neat
detail-minded
able to keep a steady hand
artistic
has good eyesight

Education and Training
Training may be acquired at vocational and technical high schools, junior and community colleges, technical institutes, or on the job.

Salary Range
$13,054–$31,004

Places of Employment
engineering firms
architecture firms
construction companies
utilities companies
government agencies

Electrician's Helper

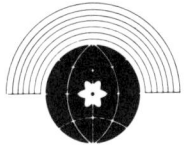

Today and Tomorrow

"Tell me it's impossible to do and I'll do it," says Sarah Smiley about the time someone tried to discourage her from enrolling in an electrician's training program by saying "women don't do things like that."

With this positive attitude, it's not so shocking to learn that Sarah, who recalls tinkering with toasters and TVs for quite some time, still tinkers—only now it's a full-time job.

As an electrician's helper, Sarah, whose workshop is the basement of a 32-floor building, has no average day. On a moment's notice, she may be replacing light bulbs or installing outlets. Whether she's up on a ladder or down on her hands and knees, turning a screwdriver or handling a sledgehammer, one thing is certain: whatever the electrical problem, Sarah carefully and patiently gets to the bottom of it. She explains that working with electricity can be dangerous.

Although Sarah truly loves her job (she claims that it was "tailor made" for her), she's quick to admit that it's not easy for a woman in this field. According to her, advancement is difficult and there's always pressure to prove yourself. But Sarah thinks women are naturals at this job. After all, she explains, they're using appliances all the time.

Sarah has hopeful words for anyone looking for a career as an electrician. "Anyone can do anything with a little encouragement. So don't think about it, do it." And she also has a reminder if the going gets rough: "There is no advantage in quitting!"

Electrician's Helper

An electrician's helper assists an electrician in the installation and repair of electrical wiring, light fixtures, and other electrical equipment. As part of the job, the electrician's helper may measure, cut, and bend wire and conduit; drill holes for wiring; and assist in lifting, positioning, and fastening objects. Minor repairs such as replacing fuses, light bulbs, and light switches are also part of the job. The electrician's tools include pipe benders, hacksaws, power drills, and other hand tools.

Special Qualities
able to work well with hands
mechanically minded
knowledgeable about safety rules
agile
physically fit

Education and Training
On-the-job training or a formal apprenticeship program are equally good ways to train.

Salary Range
$10,000–$16,000

Places of Employment
manufacturing firms
utilities companies
government agencies

Engineer

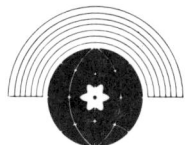

Today and Tomorrow

The words "early warning fire detection system" may not ring a bell for everyone, but they do for Kathryn Gavin. She's been designing plans to install six of them.

As an engineer, Kathryn works on one project at a time. Right now, she's updating fire detection systems for six city buildings, old and new, ranging in height from 14 floors to 40. She begins by visiting each building and surveying and recording the equipment already on each floor, basement, and roof. Then, she returns to her office and draws up the new plan using the notes she has marked directly on the building blueprints. Once the plans are complete (with the assistance of the drafter), it's Kathryn who oversees the builders and electricians who actually install the system.

Even if she hasn't installed a system with her own hands, when that "little square on a piece of paper finally becomes reality," that's a good feeling for Kathryn. But the paperwork that goes with it—that she can live without.

For a girl who chose a profession simply by looking through a career book, Kathryn has some complicated future plans. She's getting a degree in urban planning and hoping for a promotion, too. And after getting all this building experience, her next ambition is to study architecture.

If you're considering engineering as a profession, Kathryn recommends beginning your blueprint early. As a start, she suggests working on a building maintenance crew, in a drafting firm, or even as a flag person on a construction crew. Kathryn herself began by working for a surveyor, knee deep in the snow.

Engineer

An engineer is an inventor. She/he analyzes mechanical systems and products and tries to design more efficient ways they can work. After analyzing a problem by collecting and studying related information, the engineer may draw plans, construct models, and design experiments to find solutions. An engineer works with a team of scientists, drafters, and technicians on a variety of projects: bridges, skyscrapers, medical apparatus, artificial organs, scientific research instruments, and household appliances. There are more than 25 fields in which an engineer may specialize.

Special Qualities
analytical
able to work with others
creative
detail-minded
skilled in oral and written communication
mathematics-oriented

Education and Training
A bachelor's degree is the minimum requirement for any beginning job.

Salary Range
$24,132–$79,021

Places of Employment
engineering firms
utilities companies
construction companies
colleges and universities
government agencies

Flight Attendant

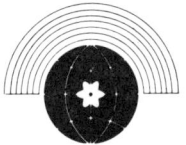

Today and Tomorrow

Every career has its ups and downs, you may think. But according to Sandy Muñoz, flight attendant, "There's nothing about my job that I don't like." And, she adds, "There's more to the job than many people think."

The passengers on her airplane don't see all the skills Sandy learned in her flight attendant training program. And she hopes they never will! As part of her training, Sandy has been taught exactly what to do in critical situations like unexpected landings or medical emergencies. It's not responding to these emergencies that scares Sandy, however. "Speaking before all those passengers makes my knees rattle." She explains that before takeoff she must use the public address system to instruct the passengers on the use of safety equipment and to point out the locations of the emergency exits. When this task is complete, Sandy feels very much at ease serving food, passing out pillows or magazines, and even just chatting with passengers.

It's not surprising that Sandy meets a lot of famous people including politicians, movie stars, and musicians who travel often. Recently, in fact, a well-known singer repaid the entire airline crew for making his flight so pleasant. He sent a limousine to pick them up and chauffeur them to his performance, followed by dinner and a dockside party on a yacht!

Flight attendants work only part of each week, and according to Sandy that's one of the best advantages of the job. "I have so much free time to do other things." Sometimes weather conditions delay a return flight, and that gives Sandy additional time to spend in different cities and to pursue her latest hobby—reading.

For someone who wasn't used to a rigid schedule, Sandy had to make a major change in her way of life on the very first day she reported for work as a flight attendant. "I never did so much planning ahead," she confesses. "But can you imagine what would happen if I didn't arrive on time for a flight!"

Flight Attendant

A flight attendant works aboard a commercial passenger plane to make the flight safe, comfortable, and enjoyable. Before each flight, the attendant sees that the cabin is in order, and checks that supplies, emergency equipment, food, and beverages are on board. As passengers enter the plane, the flight attendant greets them, checks tickets, and helps passengers store small pieces of luggage. Before takeoff, the attendant instructs passengers in the use of emergency equipment and checks to see that seat belts are fastened. Other job duties include helping to care for small children and elderly and disabled passengers, answering questions, serving beverages and precooked meals, and distributing magazines.

Special Qualities

poised
tactful
able to communicate well
resourceful
healthy
able to handle emergency situations

Education and Training

Commercial airline training programs or training at private airline schools are ways to prepare for this career.

Salary Range

$12,500–$35,000

Places of Employment

commercial passenger airlines

Geologist

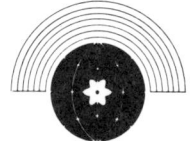

Today and Tomorrow

Vivien Gornitz used to love collecting rocks, minerals, and shells in her own backyard as a hobby. Years later, in college and as a graduate student, Vivien continued collecting, only this time she traveled a little further to study specimens from the Grand Canyon and even the Dead Sea. Today, as a geologist, Vivien Gornitz is still collecting, still studying, and still enjoying.

In her most recent position, Vivien has moved out of the field and into an office. Now, at a space science center, she studies the earth from a distance, using data and photographs taken by satellite. With this technique (called remote sensing), Vivien can locate mineral resources, pinpoint cracks in the earth, inventory worldwide crop yields, and even detect changes in water quality.

Vivien remarks that in the last ten years there has been a "revolution" in geology. And she's glad to be part of it. In the 1960s, when landing on the moon became a reality, she was into lunar geology. Now, it's remote sensing. And tomorrow, Mars!

Yet, even with all this excitement, things can get pretty lonely at times. As Vivien explains, "Research is isolating." Right now, she's working on an individual project so there is little opportunity to share her work (and her excitement) with other geologists. However, Vivien recognizes that some people prefer working alone, while others do better in teams. And both are possible in the field of geology.

If you're interested in geology, Vivien suggests taking all the math, chemistry, and physics courses you can. Then, in college, you must be willing to work hard and miss out on some fun every now and then. And when you finally make it, whether you're studying uranium mines in the Grand Canyon or moon rocks in a laboratory, you'll find it fascinating to be in a field where "big things are happening."

Geologist

A geologist studies the composition, history, and structure of the earth and, more recently, of the moon and other planets. Some geologists spend most of their time in the field where they collect and study rocks, minerals, and fossils. But many more work in labs or research centers closely examining specimens and data obtained from the field.

Special Qualities
interested in outdoor activities
curious
analytical
skilled in oral and written communication
willing to travel

Education and Training
A master's degree is usually required for most positions, although a bachelor's degree may be adequate in a few cases. For research, a doctorate is required.

Salary Range
$14,822–$50,000

Places of Employment
industries (petroleum and natural gas companies, mining and quarrying companies)
research firms
federal government (U.S. Geological Survey)
colleges and universities
natural history museums

Insurance Salesperson

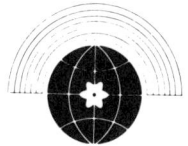

Today and Tomorrow

"Computer foul-ups aren't all bad," says Ciony Clemente about her introduction to a career in life insurance sales. As she explains, "I once received a letter stating that I hadn't paid my insurance premium when I knew I had." Furious, Ciony marched into the sales office, took her case to the general manager, and hours later, waltzed out with an apology and a job offer, too.

As a life insurance salesperson, Ciony begins each Monday in her office telephoning clients to schedule appointments for the week. On an average, she arranges two or three meetings with clients a day, sometimes in the afternoon, other times in the evening; some local, some long distance; some lasting one hour, others two. Out of all these appointments, her goal is simply two sales each week.

At this pace, Ciony has earned a comfortable income and ten company awards in just two and a half years. Obviously, satisfaction came quickly for Ciony who began in the "rookie room" sharing a desk and telephone. She quickly moved to an office of her own, and was even sent out of town on an all-expense-paid educational seminar. But there were low points along the way. Ciony recalls visiting clients on cold winter nights to make a sale, only to be turned down.

Looking ahead, Ciony sees a promotion to the assistant manager level where she'll step out of sales and into recruiting. In the more distant future, she envisions managing an entire office of her own.

Summing up her position, Ciony says, "In this business, you set your own goals, use your own system, and no one tells you what to do. You can do as much or as little as you want, but the pressure comes from within." Ciony admits that financially insurance is a "risky business." But she quickly adds, "If you're knowledgeable and confident, that's the best insurance you can have."

Insurance Salesperson

An insurance agent sells policies that protect people and businesses from future losses. The most common policies are life insurance, health insurance, and casualty insurance (covering losses from auto accidents, fire, theft, etc.). While some time is spent in the office maintaining records and preparing reports, the bulk of an agent's work is discussing insurance policies directly with customers.

Special Qualities
skilled in oral and written communication
self-confident
able to take initiative
enthusiastic

Education and Training
A bachelor's degree is preferred, but many companies will hire high school graduates with related work experience. All agents, however, must be licensed in the state where they plan to sell insurance.

Salary Range
$12,000–$100,000+
(Most agents work on a commission basis.)

Places of Employment
insurance companies
independent insurance agencies

Marine Biologist

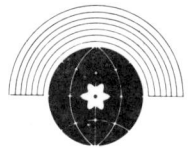

Today and Tomorrow

Evie Kallman never really had just one career in mind. As she says, "I always wanted to be everything rolled into one." Today, at age 25, Evie is a teacher, a student, a scientist, and a scuba diver. And if that sounds fishy, you're right. Evie Kallman is a marine biologist.

As a Ph.D. candidate and researcher, Evie spends most of her time in a laboratory with over 3,000 fish-filled aquariums. After feeding her fish (dog food) and cleaning some tanks, Evie is ready for more serious business—fin transplants or thyroid tumor tests. Then there is always time out for a special hello to Jack Dempsy, her pet fish.

In addition to her research, Evie teaches three biology classes at a university. She is also employed every now and then as an environmental consultant, when she may be asked, for example, to study the impact building plans may have on endangered marine wildlife such as the bog turtle.

But the best part of the job for this marine biologist is scooping up specimens from the ocean. According to Evie, who even "dives for dinner," it's really beautiful down there. She describes the sea as "a world apart." Evie's quick to add, though, that there are dangers (the possibility of sharks) and uncomfortable conditions. For instance, in 20-degree rainy weather, when you're on a boat and the wind is blowing, "30 layers of clothing won't keep you warm."

Obviously, the discomforts don't stop Evie, and they don't have to stop you either. In Evie's view, if you have the inclination and if you're bright, hardy, and like the outdoors, a career in marine biology may be the perfect catch for you.

Marine Biologist

A marine biologist specializes in the study of saltwater marine life. A limnologist studies freshwater marine life. Both scientists study the plants and animals living in the water, and the environmental conditions, both man-made and natural, that affect them.

Special Qualities
physically fit
hardy
skilled in oral and written communication
curious
analytical
willing to travel

Education and Training
A bachelor's degree in biology or a related field is the minimum requirement for a beginning job. However, advanced degrees are usually required for jobs in research and teaching.

Salary Range
$12,000–$45,000

Places of Employment
colleges and universities
government agencies
fish laboratories

Stockbroker

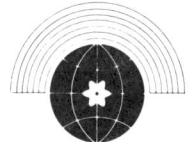

Today and Tomorrow

As far back as she can recall, Amy Lampert remembers thinking that she would grow up, get married, and have children. But she got sidetracked along the way. Some 20 years later, Amy has not yet married, has no children, and has no immediate plans for either.

As a busy stockbroker, Amy spends each day prospecting for new customers and advising and assisting her ongoing clients in the buying and selling of their stocks. She also does a lot of telephone work (about 100 calls a day), a considerable amount of paperwork, and keeps a constant watch on the news and numbers. As Amy explains, "There's no news in the world that doesn't affect the stock market—from presidential elections to new breakfast cereals." This explains why Amy begins each day reading newspapers from headlines to fine print. And it also accounts for the compact computers in her office flashing numbers to her right, news to her left.

Using the newest news and numbers to advise her clients successfully pays big dividends in the personal satisfaction department. But when Amy hasn't done well for a client, she says, "That can be devastating." She's quick to add, however, "Errors don't happen too often, thank goodness!"

In an atmosphere that switches from high pressure to low, from fast paced to slow, from noisy to silent, Amy finds that you must be persistent, consistent, and willing to work hard. Amy believes you don't have to be a math whiz to succeed in this business, but an outgoing personality is "an added plus."

To the occasional client who remarks, "A female stockbroker! What next?" Amy doesn't hesitate to answer. "Management, of course." Looking ahead, Amy sees leaving her clients behind to manage and teach other brokers.

Stockbroker

A stockbroker (also called a securities salesworker) handles the buying and selling of stocks and bonds for clients. She/he offers clients financial counseling, furnishes information about the advantages and disadvantages of a particular investment, and supplies the latest dollar figures for stocks and bonds. A beginning stockbroker also spends a good deal of time searching for customers to establish a clientele.

Special Qualities

able to communicate well
self-confident
informed
ambitious
observant
analytical
able to work independently

Education and Training

A bachelor's degree is preferred. On-the-job training is required for all positions.

Salary Range

$12,000–$50,000+
(Most agents work on a commission basis.)

Places of Employment

securities firms

Telephone Installer

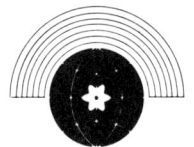

Today and Tomorrow

In a family where both parents are electrical engineers, it's not surprising that Ruth Whitesell grew up playing with electric trains and building model engines and radios. Nor is it so shocking to learn that Ruth chose a career installing telephones in residential homes. "There were no restrictions in my mind," Ruth recalls when she applied for a job as the only female telephone installer on a "gang" of 12 men.

In the morning, Ruth checks in at her station to check out her assignments. And after that, she's on her own with a drill, hammer, and staple gun as her only companions. The agenda may consist of just one major job, or seven minor ones. Ruth explains that in this business a simple job is plugging a phone into a line. But a complex job may mean running wire across a 30-foot ceiling, along a roof, into a backyard, or through a basement.

In a job that seems so mechanical, there's some human interest, too. Ruth meets lots of people, sometimes famous ones. She recalls the times she installed phones for a well-known newscaster and a famous movie actress. But being a telephone installer isn't all glamour. There are basement rats and fleas, and sometimes unfamiliar neighborhoods to visit. Yet knowing that she (or any other installer) can call for backup help at any time is all the comfort she needs.

How does Ruth feel about doing a job that's traditionally male? "It's fun. I get a laugh out of it, and so do customers!" Ruth remembers the time she knocked on a customer's door. A lady answered and yelled to her husband, "Herbie, come here. You won't believe this! The telephone man—it's a lady!"

Telephone Installer

A telephone installer travels (most often by truck) to customers' homes and offices to install new phones, remove old ones, or make changes in existing equipment; for example, changing the model or color of the phone, or adding an extension. In homes, installing a new phone often requires climbing poles to get to outside service wires. In apartment buildings, however, wires can be connected in the basement.

Special Qualities

has good eyesight and color perception
mechanically minded
physically fit

Education and Training

Telephone companies provide both classroom instruction and on-the-job training.

Salary Range

$10,000–$22,000

Places of Employment

telephone companies

Actress

Arts

At the age of 16, Shirley Blanc saw a dancer performing in a poor neighborhood. "This affected my whole life and made me want to be a performer," she recalls. In preparation for her stage career she studied dance, majored in drama in college, and tried out for all kinds of roles to get experience. Eventually, she found exciting acting assignments in the theater, television, movies, and educational films.

Her career was somewhat altered by marriage and raising children. Since she could not travel for long periods of time or work in the evening due to family responsibilities, she did mostly television work, drama and poetry readings, educational films, and teaching. Now that her children are grown, her interest in the theater has become more active, and she appears in productions on Broadway, Off Broadway, and even Off Off Broadway.

"The life of an actress is not easy," admits Shirley. "You must be in good health, top working condition, determined, constantly improving your craft, looking your best, and able to work with others. As an actress you must also be disciplined because there is a very limited amount of time to achieve what you want—a typical Broadway show has four weeks of 12-hour-a-day rehearsals just prior to opening."

"To become a good actress," advises Shirley, "don't shut yourself off to experience. Concentrate on and observe people. Use yourself as a resource: openness to life is the artist's material and you must choose your own unique approach because the source of everything is inside you."

Actress

An actress brings a character to life for an audience—a good actress will be able to portray many types of people from all walks of life. She spends long hours working and rehearsing, often must travel, and is required to memorize many pages of script. An actress may work in an acting company, a repertory group, on the stage, on television or radio, and in motion pictures, most often with a team of other performers under a single director. She may play the leading character, a supporting role, an "extra" (who delivers no lines), or serve as an understudy.

Special Qualities
able to portray characters convincingly
able to concentrate
able to memorize
resilient
creative
poised
dedicated

Education and Training
Training either in a school of dramatic arts, or at a college or university which has a drama curriculum, or with a drama coach, is desirable.

Salary Range
$5,000-$100,000+
(Many paying jobs are available only on a part-time basis.)

Places of Employment

theater companies	radio stations
film companies	advertising agencies (commercials)
television stations	drama schools

Architect

Arts

Trudi Rosen had completed her training and worked as an architect for seven years before she retired temporarily to raise her children. She's glad to have had some time away from the drawing board, however, because she was able to achieve objectivity toward her work, and to grow professionally by reading and keeping in contact with other architects. When she returned to work ten years later, she was able to pick up where she had left off.

Today, Trudi is a busy architect concentrating on building restoration and landscape architecture. On an average workday she may be visiting jobs in progress, checking buildings to see that they meet both safety and design standards, sketching, drafting, drawing up contracts, billing clients, taking competitive bids, keeping in touch with resource people, reading journals, and keeping clients up-to-date on work in progress.

"Two characteristics most needed in this work are enormous energy and love of hard work," says Trudi. "I find my work very demanding, but also rewarding. I hope never to retire, because architecture is a profession where age is not a handicap—architects improve with age, and many work well into their 90s."

Tracing the roots of her interest in architecture, Trudi speaks of her mother who, though not an architect, had redone the interiors and landscaping of the apartment building she owned. Architecture school offered a special challenge, Trudi notes, because of its individualized workshop approach and the chance for a lot of interaction with instructors.

Trudi concludes, "Most exciting to me is having the know-how to make the world a better place to live in and perhaps to affect the quality of life." Her designs and renovations for parks, playgrounds, medical centers, apartment houses, and office buildings are probably doing just that.

Architect

An architect designs buildings including homes, hospitals, schools, museums, offices, factories, and theaters. She/he works with clients to determine space requirements; to discuss costs; and to design, restore, or renovate buildings which will meet people's needs. An architect must be knowledgeable about government regulations that affect building designs, building materials, lighting, heating, and health and safety standards. Once the building is designed, the architect works with contractors to carry out the building plan.

Special Qualities

visual
artistic
interested in improving the environment
skilled in mathematics
creative
patient

Education and Training

A bachelor's degree or a master's degree in architecture is necessary. A three-year internship with a licensed architect is usually required. Then the architect may take a state licensing exam to show she/he is competent to practice in the field and to protect the public health, welfare, and safety.

Salary Range

$16,200–$50,000+

Places of Employment

architecture firms
colleges and universities
consulting firms
government agencies

Art Director

Arts

Elissa Querze trained for ten years to be a concert pianist, but her hobby was always drawing. When the time came to find a career, Elissa chose advertising because of her interest in graphic arts. Her studies at an art institute convinced her that her greater talents were in art, not in music. She has not regretted her decision to switch to the visual arts field.

Today, Elissa is one of the few women art directors in the medical advertising field. At the agency where Elissa works, the pace is rushed. "Under stress I hang in there—I take lots of vitamins and do yoga to keep calm," says Elissa. She must make many decisions each day as she handles projects for different clients who use the agency. Her tasks are varied. She creates new concepts and ways to express them visually; selects paper stock, color, and type; attends photography shootings; chooses photos for use in her ads; checks proofs; and supervises the preparation of layouts. She also meets with clients, discusses concepts with staff, makes budget estimates, and hires free-lance artists.

As successful as Elissa is, she confides, "As a woman my progress has been slower when it came to promotions. It's slower for women who have abilities equal to men to move up the advertising career ladder." It is rare for a woman to have overall control of the marketing of a product.

Elissa's advice for someone entering the field is: "After completing your education, take any job in advertising to get a foothold, and then work your way up from there. Remember that advertising is the melding of both visual and verbal ideas, and that the ability to work well with people is crucial in this field."

Art Director

The art director creates concepts and designs layouts for advertisements for newspapers, magazines, posters, billboards, and direct mail brochures. After the layout is sketched, the art director prepares samples called comprehensives which are submitted to the client for approval. Based on discussion with the client, the art director estimates costs and makes final choices of paper, color scheme, and type. In many cases, she/he will hire free-lance artists and photographers to execute the artwork for the ad. The art director sees the project through to completion, including supervising photography and checking proofs and mechanicals.

Special Qualities

visual
creative
artistic
able to work well under pressure
able to work well with others

Education and Training

Three or four years of training at a specialized art school, or a bachelor's degree with a major in art, is required.

Salary Range

$10,000-$40,000+

Places of Employment

advertising agencies
department stores
graphic arts studios
businesses and industries (advertising departments)

Ceramicist

Arts

"I like to work with my hands. By being playful with materials and experimenting with shapes, an idea grows. It's always a surprise when I see a new, finished piece. It gives me a sense of satisfaction and I can't wait to start the next piece," Hilda Stekel happily observes from her studio equipped with kiln, potter's wheel, tools, and clay.

Hilda describes the process for making a ceramic piece. The necessary supplies and equipment are purchased as the first step. There are many kinds of clay, glazes, and chemicals that can be used, and the ceramic artist selects those combinations that best fit the design she/he wishes to create. The clay is then prepared—it is kneaded and wedged to rid it of air bubbles, and always kept moist. It may be thrown on the potter's wheel or built up, modeled or carved. Whatever method is used, the piece must be free of air bubbles or it will explode inside the kiln (oven). After a piece has been thrown or hand-built, it is air-dried, sometimes for a week or longer. "I've lost pieces when I haven't been patient and waited for them to dry long enough," Hilda recalls. After the piece is dried thoroughly, it is fired in a kiln and later glazed.

Hilda has been commissioned to do many pieces of ceramic sculpture for private homes and gardens. She will usually fire the sculpture in small parts and then put them together as a large piece. Describing these large sculptures, Hilda says, "I find these a challenge because they are more complex and make more of an artistic statement. They bring ceramics into the field of sculpture more than pottery does. On a large ceramic sculpture, I discover what I want to express and how creative I can be with a piece of clay." Her words tell a lot about the joys of being a ceramicist.

Ceramicist

Ceramics is a broad term that includes both pottery and ceramic sculpture. A ceramicist is an artist who designs combinations of forms, textures, and colors and translates those into the medium of clay. She/he must know the temperatures used to fire different clays as well as the glazes that work best on each type of clay. Ceramicists shape their pieces on a potter's wheel or by hand. Their works are sold in shops or made at the request of individuals.

Special Qualities

artistic
able to work well with hands
sensitive to design, color, and texture
interested in chemistry
patient
able to do heavy physical work
able to market one's products

Education and Training

College is not necessary. A ceramicist can apprentice in a studio or take courses and workshops in a craft school or other facility. However, a study of art, design, and history of art on a college level will help develop a ceramicist's career potential.

Salary Range

$8,000–$18,000+

Places of Employment

art studios
craft schools
schools, colleges, and universities
industries
self-employment

Conductor

Arts

"I've played the piano since age five. I feel lucky that my joy is in music. To be a performer you have to be tough. It means continuing your work against frustration and rejection. Very few women ever try to be conductors," says Eve Queler while a group of opera singers rehearses nearby.

As a conductor, Eve has led orchestras in cities throughout the United States as well as in Montreal, London, Barcelona, and Paris. She founded and directs her own orchestra and has won many awards for her work. Eve attributes some of her success to the support and encouragement of her husband and two children who have believed in her work throughout her years of struggle as one of the few female conductors in the United States.

When Eve is not guest conducting, she is researching seldom-played operas, casting and rehearsing opera singers, ordering music, fund raising, performing administrative tasks, and making recordings. Her work often takes her around the world. She may be studying musical scores in Paris or in Washington, D.C., in order to bring the most superb music she can to her audiences. Eve has conducted rarely performed operas by Verdi, Donizetti, and Massenet.

In a job almost completely dominated by men, Eve has proven that ability is a key factor for success. But, she acknowledges, "You have to persevere, stay with what you believe, be willing to sacrifice for long-range goals, struggle for perfection, face loneliness and rejection—and overcome. You have to be made of very strong stuff to be a female conductor," she concludes. And Eve Queler certainly is!

Conductor

A conductor leads a musical group such as an orchestra, dance band, or choral group. The conductor auditions musicians and selects them according to the type of music to be performed. She/he directs the tone, harmonic balance, tempo, rhythm, and range of the instruments. By knowing a great deal about the instruments, the talents of the musicians, and the musical composition, the conductor tries to create a harmonious blending of all these ingredients.

Special Qualities

sensitive to and knowledgeable about music
interested in trying out new interpretations of music
determined
able to lead
precise
patient

Education and Training

Specialized training at a music school with courses in conducting, or a bachelor's degree in music, is desirable.

Salary Range

$10,000-$100,000+
(Many paying jobs are available only on a part-time basis.)

Places of Employment

symphony orchestras
community and college/university orchestras
television stations
bands
music schools

Dancer

Arts

Mary Hinkson has been dancing since she was a little girl. "I danced constantly, even though I thought I wanted to be a nurse," she says. As a member of a major modern dance company, Mary feels strongly about the challenge of her career. "Dancing is so demanding; it is an enormous commitment of time and energy; it is discipline forever. If you have an irrepressible wish to move and dance, seek training as early as possible with the best teacher for your talents. A college degree is not needed, but good dance training is." Mary feels her most frustrating experience as a dancer was when an injury or illness kept her from performing.

Mary majored in physical education in college, but she disliked sports classes. Somehow, she stumbled into the dance program to meet the degree requirements, and there she found her life's work. Now, after 25 years of world tours, television appearances, and theater performances, Mary can look back at the "long hours, insecurity, and low pay" in the early years of her career in the field of modern dance when she had to teach to exist. For her, dancing was a seven-day-a-week job, and holidays were unheard of. But she did take off six weeks when her daughter was born.

Mary speaks fondly of her first dance teacher, a woman now in her 80s, who once remarked, "Dance is bodies moving beautifully, not beautiful bodies moving." Mary feels that the sense of values she learned as a student made it possible for her to overcome the hardships of her first years in the competitive world of dance. "I kept before me the vision of loving dance, the dedication, inner strength, and belief in myself as a unique human being instilled in me by a great teacher who encouraged me to concentrate on the totality of dance."

Dancer

A dancer uses body movement to express the story and emotions of a musical composition. Dance takes many forms including ballet, modern, folk, jazz, and tap. Dancers often perform in teams with selected soloists. The long hours of strenuous training, exercise, and practice require good health and great physical stamina. A dancer may also work out the dance movements (choreograph) to a musical composition.

Special Qualities
interested in dance and movement
graceful
determined
healthy
self-disciplined
physically fit

Education and Training
A dancer almost always begins training as a child. The number of years required depends on the student's development. A bachelor's degree is not essential, but a study of music, literature, and drama is valuable.

Salary Range
$5,000–$100,000+
(Many paying jobs are available only on a part-time basis.)

Places of Employment
dance companies
dance schools
theater companies
colleges and universities
hospitals and rehabilitation centers
community recreation centers

Fashion Designer

Arts

Betsy Gonzalez came to the United States from Puerto Rico when she was three years old. And even then she had her career in sight. "I always wanted to be an artist," says Betsy. "Even before I could talk or write, I could draw." As proof of her skill, Betsy won 13 gold medals in fine arts before she completed high school.

Art came very easily to Betsy in those days—and it still does. Today she is a fashion designer and head of her own company. And Betsy is still winning awards for her work. In fact, she recently won not one but two of fashion's most honored awards.

After high school, Betsy went to a school of design where she majored in fashion. Following graduation, she worked for a number of different fashion designers. Her work took her to many far-away places—Hong Kong, Bangkok, Paris, London, Athens. These experiences not only broadened her interest in history and world cultures, they also provided many sources of inspiration for her prolific designs.

Betsy's career path has not always been smooth. Establishing her own business meant taking risks and being willing to give up her security to "cut out a space" for herself. Being her own boss also means that Betsy is responsible for the business details of her work, including bill paying, studying "the market," and overseeing production from pattern making to finishing touches. But the pressure and the pace have their rewards too, especially when Betsy gets to advertise her own ideas by wearing clothes that once existed only in her imagination.

Betsy believes that a fashion designer should help a woman develop her own style. A designer should give a woman the "tools" to create her own "look." Says Betsy, "I don't design for women who want to be 'dressed.' I make clothes for women who want new ways to use their imagination. My separates encourage the wearer to try out various combinations. Each one is a different outfit. That way, my clothes are constantly new!" So is Betsy's enthusiasm for her chosen career!

Fashion Designer

A fashion designer creates new types and styles of wearing apparel and accessories. Inspiration for a new design may come from a variety of experiences: observing lifestyles, seeing the work of other designers, observing new fabrics, or traveling. A designer needs both creativity and practical knowledge of the apparel business so that she/he can translate her/his ideas into styles that can be produced at competitive prices. The designer starts by drawing sketches and selecting fabrics, trim, and colors. These sketches are used to make an experimental dress (coat, suit, blouse, etc.). Then this sample is adjusted on a form or live model. Once the design is approved, a pattern maker works closely with the designer to turn the sample into a master pattern for manufacture.

Special Qualities

creative
dedicated
imaginative
sensitive to design, texture, and color
business-minded
interested in fashion trends

Education and Training

Three to four years of training in art and fashion at a school of design is required. Following school, an apprenticeship in a firm is a good way to gain practical experience.

Salary Range

$15,000–$100,000+

Places of Employment

fashion design firms
clothing manufacturers
self-employment

Foreign Correspondent

Arts

Marguerite Cartwright's life as a foreign correspondent, professor of political science, and even movie star has been exciting and unique. As a young woman working in professional theater, she had a starring role in a Hollywood film. After making pictures, Marguerite returned to the east and went to school at night, working as a social worker during the day. She completed her doctorate in political science, and taught at a large city university. Then she began writing a column for a local newspaper, was invited to cover an important conference in Indonesia, and has been writing and visiting all over the world ever since.

Marguerite has covered stories in Burma, England, France, Ghana, Israel, Japan, Liberia, Mexico, Nigeria, Russia, Singapore, the West Indies, and many more spots around the globe. She has flown more than 300,000 miles and visited more than 100 countries, a number of them many times. There's even a street named after her in Nigeria, and a Marguerite Cartwright Bridge in the country of Xenia built by Peace Corps volunteers in her honor.

"There's more to journalism than glamour," claims Marguerite. She feels a foreign correspondent needs excellent health, energy, initiative, and an understanding of the world. The foreign correspondent must be able to cover a variety of stories including disasters or wars. The problem of finding interpreters and the pressure to write quickly and mail stories out are only some of the frustrations faced by overseas correspondents.

Marguerite finds that her career field has changed because today there are overseas news bureaus that station people around the globe to cover stories. News is wired back from overseas desks and sent around the world. Currently, Marguerite is a United Nations press corps reporter. In this job, she continues her important work covering a range of topics such as early childhood education, civil rights legislation, the women's movement, African affairs, and the Middle East.

Foreign Correspondent

A foreign correspondent reports news and feature stories for television and radio stations, newspapers, and news syndicates. Stationed in a distant country, she/he collects and analyzes newsworthy information, does research, and conducts interviews. All this material is then quickly translated into well-written, readable articles to be delivered to the home office by telephone, mail, radio, or even telegraph. Some foreign correspondents do live coverage on television, bringing world events close to home.

Special Qualities
skilled in oral and written communication
appreciative of various cultures
multilingual
able to take initiative
energetic
healthy

Education and Training
A bachelor's degree with a broad background in sociology, political science, economics, psychology, and history, plus a master's degree in one of these areas or in journalism, are required.

Salary Range
$12,000–$55,000

Places of Employment
newspapers
magazines
press wire services
television stations
radio stations

Illustrator

Arts

Stella Warwick began drawing pictures in kindergarten and, as early as that, her teachers told her mother that she had "special talent" and should plan to go to art school.

Later, Stella did indeed win a scholarship to art school. She worked her way through school with part-time jobs in department stores, window display, photo coloring, and even as a waitress. When she graduated, she taught art for four years at the school where she had studied. Now, years later, Stella does commercial art for newspapers, magazines, posters, brochures, billboards, advertisements, books, and filmstrips.

Commercial artists work with specifications such as size, number of pages, amount of copy, type styles, and color scheme. "It's always a great feeling when you've succeeded in doing a job that pleases both the client and yourself," says Stella. Her studio is filled with the tools of her trade—paintbrushes, colored inks, watercolors, tempera paints, rulers, poster boards, sketchbooks, and paper of all sizes and colors. She surrounds herself with samples of her inventive artwork, from brightly colored tissue drawings to rough sketches in black-and-white.

Stella suggests that an aspiring illustrator get a strong background in the arts and gain the technical knowledge needed. As she says, "Keep working at your art and keep your standards high. Don't be afraid of new challenges in the art field; but consider each challenge an opportunity to grow, a way to stretch yourself, even if you've never done it before."

Illustrator

An illustrator creates pictures, diagrams, and ornamental designs for books, magazines, advertisements, record album covers, billboards, posters, and catalogs. Using the specifications set by the client, the illustrator selects a medium (watercolor, pastel, tempera, pen-and-ink) and draws rough sketches. After these sketches are approved, the illustrator executes the artwork in final form.

Special Qualities

sensitive to form, color, and design
imaginative
visual
able to do finely detailed artwork
self-motivated
patient

Education and Training

A bachelor's degree in fine arts or training at an art school is highly desirable. Some illustrators are self-taught.

Salary Range

$10,000–$50,000+

Places of Employment

art studios
department stores
industries (fashion houses, film companies, greeting card companies, catalog houses, publishers)
colleges and universities
art schools
self-employment

Interior Designer

Arts

Eugenie Young began college as a chemistry major, but she remembers how she always loved to draw. She used to turn all her school projects, from writing to science, into art projects. "Being a chemistry major wasn't for me," reports Eugenie, "so I left college and got married. But after a while I felt restless and decided to go back to school. This time I majored in art—something I *really* wanted to learn about."

After finishing her courses in interior design, Eugenie found it necessary to apprentice for a while at a low salary. Then she got a job at a small design studio, and was soon promoted to chief designer. With the knowledge of business and clients she had gained, she decided to move up the career ladder and start her own interior design firm.

Although a little frightened at first, Eugenie, with the support of her husband and clients, launched the business and has been happy about her decision ever since. "I love my work. Interior decorating is a form of personal expression for each client, and the good interior designer is sensitive to how a person's living environment will affect her/his mental outlook and daily life. Because I'm a 'people person,' I enjoy working with clients, drafters, manufacturers, contractors, salespeople, carpenters, painters, and carpet layers."

Eugenie's work involves assessing her client's needs, selecting samples, getting prices, supervising contractors, and working at her drawing board. "When I place a blank piece of paper on the drawing board, I am amazed at the ideas that pour forth," claims Eugenie. Then she translates her ideas into a scale drawing and makes decisions about color, furnishing, and accessories. "These ideas are all executed by craftspeople whom I respect. Without them, no idea can come to life."

Interior Designer

An interior designer plans the methods to decorate and furnish the rooms in homes, offices, and commercial buildings. She/he works with clients to help them select furnishings and accessories based on the clients' personal needs, tastes, and budgets. The designer selects samples, checks prices, and visits suppliers. Then scale drawings are developed for approval by the client. Finally, the interior designer implements the plans by making purchases; arranging for delivery of items; and subcontracting with painters, carpenters, upholsterers, etc.

Special Qualities

sensitive to the needs and desires of others
artistic
able to coordinate the activities of others
able to work well with others
business-minded
visual

Education and Training

Training at a two-year art school or institute of interior design, or a bachelor's degree in architecture or interior design, is highly desirable. Some correspondence programs are also offered.

Salary Range

$15,200–$46,500+

Places of Employment

interior design firms
architecture firms
department stores
industries (furniture and fabric companies)

Journalist-Editor

Arts

"I enjoy meeting people and I like to write—that's what my job's about," says Joan O'Sullivan, senior editor at a large newspaper syndicate.

It seems that Joan has not been without paper, pencil, or typewriter since she helped found her high school newspaper. When she was 16 she got a summer job as a copygirl for a city newspaper and used the opportunity to try her skill at finding and writing stories. She broke into print with a feature on a stranded cat; soon after she was hired as a full-time writer for the school page. When she decided to go to college, she chose an evening program so that she could still devote time to her budding career as a journalist. Joan later joined the women's page staff of a newspaper syndicate where she climbed the career ladder to become women's editor and then senior editor.

Over the years, Joan has covered stories on women in all walks of life, as well as features that range from current maternity fashions to popular dance trends. Her work includes checking clippings on potential interviews, looking at features submitted, writing her daily columns, and interviewing. "I feel fortunate to have a job," Joan admits. "Women today are doing so many fascinating things—from joining the carpenter's union to driving cross-country trucks—things they've never done before."

In her view, a potential journalist must be curious about people, able to see relationships in seemingly unrelated information, and really like people. Breaking into journalism involves learning the discipline of reporting—writing quickly and accurately and meeting deadlines. As Joan says, "Take any job you can possibly get on a newspaper to get your foot in the door. Then prove your potential as a writer by searching out stories and presenting them."

Journalist-Editor

A journalist-editor supervises and coordinates a section of a newspaper or magazine related to a specific area such as international news, business and finance, drama, gardening, sports, real estate, or fashion. She/he makes staff assignments, and may also write and edit copy and design layouts. The editor and her/his staff continually generate new ideas for articles and stories by keeping abreast of the latest developments in their topic areas. Editors can work in other media such as books and trade journals.

Special Qualities
inquisitive
skilled in oral and written communication
accurate
able to handle pressure
informed
persistent
able to work independently and with others

Education and Training
A bachelor's degree with a major in journalism is almost always essential. A master's degree in journalism may be an added plus.

Salary Range
$20,000–$70,000+

Places of Employment
newspapers
news syndicates
magazines
trade and consumer journals
businesses and industries (publications departments)

Musician

Arts

As a child, Tania Justina Leon Ferran wanted to be, as she says, "an accountant, a doctor, a psychiatrist, an astronaut, and a musician." Born in Cuba, she began to study the piano when she was four, and grew to become one of Cuba's noted musicians. When she left Cuba she knew almost no English, and although she had three degrees—in piano and music theory, accounting, and a master's degree in music education— she had to begin her education again in the United States. She is now working toward her doctorate.

Tania once substituted for a friend as piano accompanist at a well-known dance company and the director recognized her talent immediately. Now an award-winning pianist, Tania also composes music that is often included in concert repertoires. She shows her versatility in other ways as well.

She has been a guest conductor for orchestras in many parts of the world. Tania also teaches music to 200 students and leads a 52-member orchestra she helped found. Tania's work brings her in contact with musicians, students, and parents from a variety of backgrounds. Her philosophy is "through music we can help people to work together."

Her advice to an aspiring musician is: "Find a teacher who is involved and willing to share information. Believe in what you truly want to do. Think of your career as part of society, think about what you represent in your society, and determine what you as a unique person can give others. Then follow your feelings about what you plan to give to others and be sensitive to everyday life. It is not merely what kind of musician you are, but what kind of human being you are."

Musician

A musician uses an instrument to express the rhythm, harmony, and melody of a musical composition. A musician may perform as a soloist; or in a small group, ensemble, or full orchestra in theaters, concert halls, films, and on recordings. The varieties of music are infinite; some of the most familiar ones are classical, opera, contemporary, folk, blues, jazz, and rock.

Special Qualities

love of music
sensitive to sound and rhythm
interested in interpreting music
creative
dedicated
able to work well with others

Education and Training

Extensive study of a musical instrument is essential. A bachelor's degree in music or a degree from a music school is highly desirable. A graduate degree in music or post-college training at a music school is an advantage.

Salary Range

$5,000–$100,000+
(Many jobs are available only on a part-time basis.)

Places of Employment

symphony orchestras
community orchestras and music societies
television studios
schools, colleges, and universities
music schools

Photographer

Arts

Penny Coleman wanted to be a poet when she was younger, but during her college years as a literature major she became interested in photography. After graduating from college, she spent three years in a technical photography program.

Penny specialized in photojournalism and she is currently working for a major newspaper. She takes pictures that show the places, people, and things that are happening in the news. She especially enjoys learning as she meets different people and covers various events. The challenge of rushing to the scene of a story and capturing the moment both accurately and appealingly intrigues her. She prefers this style of work to that of commercial photography, where pictures are taken in studio settings (at a more leisurely pace) using arranged shots.

Penny enjoys the techniques and tools of photography. She believes a really good photographer can use a small, inexpensive camera and get an incredible range of photos if the photographer understands the principles of composition, light, color, and texture. According to Penny, "Photography is light." And, she adds, "The photographer renders her own interpretation and understanding of a good composition."

In the future, Penny would like to expand her photographic clients to include magazines and combine this with her literary background to develop photo feature stories.

Photographer

A photographer uses a camera and related equipment to take pictures for individuals, industry, the press, television, or films. The photographer's task begins with planning effective ways to portray a subject. She/he determines the lighting; arranges the props, backgrounds, and objects or people to be photographed; decides on the use of black-and-white or color film; and considers distance, focus, and sensitivity of the film. Many photographers develop and print their own pictures. To do this, they must be familiar with chemicals, paper, and timing used to obtain different effects. A knowledge of the history of photography is useful to anyone interested in pursuing this career.

Special Qualities

sensitive to good design
able to solve problems
creative
able to work well with others
hardy
attentive to detail
observant

Education and Training

A broad liberal arts college education (including courses in art and design, business management, and chemistry), followed by special technical training, is desirable. Some four-year colleges offer a major in photography. An alternative to the college route is an apprenticeship or technical training.

Salary Range

$16,600–$100,000+

Places of Employment

newspapers
magazines
television studios
advertising firms
portrait studios
fashion houses
self-employment

Playwright

Arts

Ann Early always wanted to be a writer. She married at the age of 17 and had her first of three sons soon after. As she explains, "I'm a self-educated person. I began writing out of the anger and frustration I felt at the oppression in society; I was a black woman with no money. I wrote my first book three years after I married; it was an autobiography, 500 pages long. A local children's author encouraged me to continue writing, and after a while I found that playwriting was my medium because I had a natural talent for dialogue."

After studying playwriting, Ann worked with prison inmates, using the arts to help them express their feelings. Then she applied for and received funding from her State Council on the Arts, a local arts council, an insurance company, and private contributors in order to establish a writers-in-residence group she now directs. She describes the group, which showcases the work of new playwrights, as "the only black performing arts complex in the area, serving libraries, community centers, schools, television, and radio." Since founding the group, Ann has "discovered" an 82-year-old playwright and produced her play, and has worked with a children's theater group as well.

Ann's purpose is to bridge the gap between people of different cultures, making them aware that there is a human thread that links them all together. Not only does she bring people of many cultural backgrounds together, she also seems to bring people of all ages together. The groups participating in her writing workshops range from pre-school to older adults. There are pre-teen, teen, and adult groups working on many original projects, as well as bilingual workshops for all ages.

She has some words for future playwrights. "When I was young, everyone told me how hard it was to become a playwright. Searching for glamour and a pot of gold at the end of the rainbow is a mistake! To become a playwright you have to be committed to an idea and then stick to it," says Ann.

Playwright

A playwright writes plays which are performed in theaters, on film, and on television. As the playwright develops a theme into a play, she/he considers whether it will hold the audience's interest. Using her/his understanding of how people think, feel, and interrelate, the playwright develops characters who are believable in the setting. Then the playwright puts the characters in a plot that has conflict, purpose, and resolution. The playwright must also provide stage directions for the actors and actresses, as well as descriptive details about the setting, and any other instructions needed for performance. Often the playwright is involved in rehearsals, working closely with actors, directors, and screenplay writers (for movie and TV adaptations). She/he must also sell plays or help acquire production backing.

Special Qualities
committed
sensitive to social problems
skilled in writing
insightful
sensitive to speech patterns, inflections, and colloquialisms

Education and Training
A playwright may be self-taught by studying independently. However, the traditional training route is to earn a bachelor's degree in theater arts. Beginning playwrights should consider writing for local theater companies, and should join such groups to get production experience.

Salary Range
$0–$100,000+
(Salary often depends on getting plays produced.)

Places of Employment
theater companies
film companies
television stations
self-employment

Producer

Arts

When Victoria Hershey finished college she wanted to go into the foreign service and be a diplomat. After teaching for three years in Vietnam, she discovered she didn't want the foreign service after all. She returned to the United States and worked with young artists as director of a community center in her town. But she still wasn't satisifed and decided to find a true profession for herself. She began by writing news for a large newspaper. A year later she was hired by a major television network as a newscaster where she worked for three years.

Once in the TV world, Victoria became especially interested in producing. Her first success was a weekly news program she originated. Today, her responsibilities as a TV producer include researching stories thoroughly; editing scripts; seeing that both sides of an issue are covered; making arrangements for crews to shoot the show on location; setting up time schedules; casting; and considering budget, crews, and props.

Her advice to someone interested in the field is to get a formal education; be aware of current events, the economy, and the social climate; and learn about technology. "I feel it's very important for a woman to understand TV and film technology in order to work in it. Because equipment is always changing, I need to know the most current technological information available. Someday I hope to become an independent producer of my own videotape productions for use on TV and in schools, colleges, and libraries."

"I find satisfaction in seeing individuals achieve small victories that help them to understand themselves and others better," she explains. One of her own "small victories" is a documentary she produced on domestic workers in suburbia which attracted much attention. Currently, Victoria is producing live plays at a local theater.

Producer

A producer selects materials which will educate and entertain through the media of stage, film, or television. The duties of a producer include acquiring a play suitable for performance, arranging the financial backing, and hiring the staff—director, manager, cast, and crew. The producer also sets management policies, administers the budget, makes production schedules, and helps settle disputes on the set or stage. A producer may choose to direct her/his own plays as well.

Special Qualities

interested in the dramatic arts
persistent
imaginative
business-minded
able to coordinate the activities of others
organized
able to motivate others

Education and Training

A bachelor's degree with a broad range of liberal arts courses, plus technical training in specialized areas such as television, film, or theater, are highly desirable. An apprenticeship with a producer provides valuable work experience.

Salary Range

$8,000–$100,000+

Places of Employment

television stations
film companies
theater companies
advertising agencies
audiovisual publishers

Puppeteer

Arts

"When I was little," says Carol Fijan, "my father taught me to handle hammers, saws, and other tools because he felt women should know how to use tools." These early skills have been very useful to Carol who, as a puppeteer, not only performs but also designs and constructs her own puppets.

Today she is director of a national theater of puppet arts which she helped found. The skills required to become a puppeteer are many and varied. As Carol explains, "A puppeteer should be able to talk in many voices almost simultaneously—I know around 40 different voices, and in a single performance I may use seven or eight of them." The puppeteer also needs to have extensive training in dramatics, combined with training in the visual arts (sculpture, painting, set design), and the trades (carpentry, electronics). And, of course, puppeteers have the same work routines and pressures all theater people have such as rehearsals, performances, traveling, and long hours.

Carol regrets that people too often think of puppetry as merely "artsy craftsy" rather than a serious performing art. "The Japanese Bunraku puppets and the Javanese shadow puppets have been accepted for many years as art forms, and puppetry in this country should also be accorded the dignity of a major art form," she believes.

Carol has taught puppetry to teenagers and other groups, and her puppeteers have been invited to many places to perform. Carol recalls one group of performers she had trained who gave a performance for 600 people. She had worked with these puppeteers for three years. When the show was over the audience began to applaud. During the show the performers were hidden behind a screen, and when they came out the audience saw that the puppeteers were all in wheelchairs. "At that moment," she says, "the audience screamed and shouted and applauded through their tears at the beautiful performance given by the handicapped puppeteers."

Puppeteer

A puppeteer creates dramatic presentations using small human, animal, or supernatural forms. She/he may make these puppets out of wire, fabrics, papier-mâché, or clay, and uses paints and fabrics to costume them. Often, puppets are hinged and have connecting strings or wires to allow them to move. The puppeteer will hide behind a small screen to manipulate them. Hand-puppets, however, are held up on stage to perform. A puppeteer uses different voices to play many characters on stage and to bring entertainment and enjoyment to her/his audience.

Special Qualities

sensitive to speech patterns and individual mannerisms
interested in dramatics
attentive to detail
creative
artistic

Education and Training

Training in dramatics (acting and speech) is essential. In addition, knowledge of carpentry, set design, lighting, and sound technology is valuable. Puppeteering might be learned as part of a bachelor's degree with a major in theater or drama.

Salary Range

$100–$50,000+
(Many jobs are available only on a part-time basis.)

Places of Employment

theater companies
television stations
advertising agencies (commercials)
trade shows
schools, colleges, and universities
community centers
self-employment

Athlete

Out-of-Doors

Wyomia Tyus claims that as a young girl she had "no special career in mind." Twenty-odd years and two Olympic gold medals later, Wyomia realized just how special her career as a runner was.

Although she won her first gold medal in the 100-meter dash at the age of 18, Wyomia was by no means an overnight success. In addition to a lot of legwork, there were long hours and many lessons to be learned. Typically, a daily workout for Wyomia meant running six miles in the off-season. During the spring, when most track meets take place, there was more conditioning, more running (timed over distances long and short), and more practicing, including perfecting her start and learning to lean at the tape. All this hard work and dedication paid off with her second gold medal four years later.

For Wyomia, success was gratifying, to say the least. (She was the first sprinter to win two gold medals in the same event.) But for her, satisfaction meant more than medals. It was the sheer joy of running, the chance to travel to different places, and the many friendships she made.

Yet there were bad times, too. Wyomia recalls the camping injury that almost kept her out of the running in the 1968 Olympics. And even more frustrating was an early but inevitable end to a physically demanding career.

Today, Wyomia works in the community and no longer runs competitively. Her future plans, however, aren't so far off the track. Right now she's entertaining the possibility of becoming a sports commentator or owning and operating her own track camp.

For a hopeful young athlete, Wyomia maintains that the time is right. "The opportunities are there." But, she adds that you've got to train, get in shape, and push yourself. According to Wyomia, when it comes to winning the 100-meter dash, there are no shortcuts.

Athlete

An athlete trains to compete in exercises, sports, or games requiring physical strength, agility, and stamina. The competition may be on an amateur level such as college athletics, or on a semi-professional or professional level. Training often requires daily physical workouts and practice. While most sports are seasonal (basketball, golf, softball, tennis), athletes train year-round.

Special Qualities

determined
physically fit
hardy
self-disciplined
willing to travel
agile

Education and Training

Athletes are often coached as amateurs on the college level. For professional athletes, rigorous coaching and practice continue.

Salary Range

$2,500–$100,000+

Places of Employment

professional teams
semi-professional teams
colleges and universities

Athletic Director

Out-of-Doors

When Dorrie McCaffrey was in the fifth grade, she loved to climb trees. But each time she was scolded. "Ladies don't do that!" her teacher used to say. Now, almost three decades later, Dorrie McCaffrey, athletic director, has moved into a field almost totally dominated by men. Looking back, Dorrie wonders what her fifth grade teacher would say today.

Dorrie began her career in high school teaching physical education and coaching basketball and track. Ten years and three jobs later, she was appointed athletic director at a large college. Now, her workday starts with "a thousand things to do." First she handles the routine paper work—answering mail and signing forms. Next, she caringly deals with a constant flow of students asking questions and seeking advice. Once the traffic slows down and the phone stops ringing, Dorrie works on coordinating all the business for 19 athletic teams—arranging schedules, transportation, officials, equipment, practice times, and uniforms. All these arrangements mean a lot of details to keep in mind—medical forms that have to be collected and paychecks that need to be requested to pay officials. And Dorrie teaches two swimming classes, too. So it's no wonder she is constantly making lists and writing notes to herself.

Dorrie gets a great deal of satisfaction when she knows her teams (all 19) have "good everything," including uniforms, officials, equipment, etc. But the red tape involved in getting "the best of everything" is enough to make her "tear her hair out."

What about a woman in a field traditionally dominated by men? Dorrie believes that "one's sex is not related to this job; competence is." Yet, not everyone in her field sees it that way. When there is a nationwide meeting of athletic directors, and she is one of the few women there, Dorrie explains, "I know they're thinking that maybe I'm here because the real 'A.D.' couldn't make it."

Athletic Director

An athletic director plans, schedules, and coordinates athletic events. Specifically, she/he has responsibility for team transportation, uniforms, budget, facilities, community relations, equipment, officials, and coaches. In addition, an athletic director is usually required to supervise athletic events as well as to evaluate coaches on their performance each season. Many athletic directors head a staff of physical education teachers and may also participate in fund raising.

Special Qualities

organized
skilled in oral and written communication
able to lead others
able to relate to young people
detail-minded
enthusiastic

Education and Training

A bachelor's degree with a major in physical education, sports administration, or business administration is required. In addition, several years of experience in athletics are needed.

Salary Range

$10,000–$30,000+

Places of Employment

schools, colleges, and universities

Athletic Trainer

Out-of-Doors

Claire Chin always loved athletics, but she was no superstar. She loved hanging around the gym, but she wasn't really good enough to make the team. Sounds depressing, right? Not so for Claire Chin. She decided to put her enthusiasm to work behind the scenes, volunteering as a student trainer.

This volunteer experience scored big points for Claire. Today, as a part-time college athletic trainer, Claire arrives at the practice field early to get a jump on things like filling out insurance forms and ordering supplies. Then the taping begins—ankles, knees, thumbs, and wrists. And once practice gets underway, she must constantly keep alert for injuries on the field.

Treating injuries like sprains, cuts, bruises, and heat cramps involves a lot of basic first aid. For the more serious conditions, like hyperventilation, the treatment may be simple (a brown paper bag) but, as Claire says, "You've got to keep your cool!" Claire gets a great deal of satisfaction from calming injured players with her sense of humor. What she finds unpleasant is seeing people in pain. And she's unhappy when an injured player doesn't follow her advice.

Claire explains that to be a successful athletic trainer, you need a lot of know-how (often a master's degree) as well as an interest in people. Claire adds that a sense of humor also helps: "I'm constantly teased about entering the men's locker room, but I haven't had to go in there yet!"

Athletic Trainer

The job of an athletic trainer is to prevent athletic injuries, administer first aid if an injury should occur, and carry out any rehabilitation plans prescribed by a physician. The trainer uses skills such as first aid, taping, and fitting athletic equipment all the time. In doing the job, she/he works with the team physician as well as the coaches and athletes.

Special Qualities

confident
able to handle emergency situations
able to work with others
interested in athletics
able to work well with hands

Education and Training

A bachelor's degree in athletic training is essential. Although a master's degree and/or a teaching certificate is not required, both are highly recommended.

Salary Range

School Trainer: $10,000–$25,000
Professional Trainer: $14,000–$25,000+
(Part-time positions are also available.)

Places of Employment

high schools, colleges, and universities
professional teams

Camp Director

Out-of-Doors

Beginning as a Girl Scout, Ellie Waechter worked her way up in the camping field from camper to counselor to consultant. But after 12 years in the business, Ellie's camping days came to a close. Or at least she thought so.

"In my wildest dreams I couldn't picture myself camping again," she recalls. Yet today, ten years and two children later, Ellie directs a Girl Scout camp where she works long hours during the season and loves every minute of it.

"In this business," she explains, "it's never the same two days in a row." But there are always certain things she can count on, like the paperwork Ellie describes as "unreal." Then there are regular staff meetings, a few parent phone calls, periods of instant decision making, and a daily trot through camp.

In the top camp position, Ellie directs a staff of 35, and during the season she's responsible for nearly 700 campers (150 at a time). But Ellie sees her main role as the camp counselor's counselor. Seeing these counselors grow and develop year after year is Ellie's main source of satisfaction. And, in fact, recruiting good counselors in the first place isn't always easy.

In an atmosphere full of fresh air and fun, there are tense moments, too. Ellie recalls the night the entire camp awaited Hurricane Belle in the dining hall, and the late patrol that finally made it back before dark.

In addition to camp director training, Ellie suggests a variety of experiences in a variety of jobs and camps as the best preparation for a career as camp director. As she remarks, "You have to be ready to step in for anyone, to do anything, anywhere, at any time! And that takes experience—lots of it."

Camp Director

A camp director plans and directs a resident- or day-camp program. Her/his responsibilities generally include planning and coordinating camp activities, supervising camp staff, preparing reports, observing and enforcing health and safety measures, handling the camp budget, and maintaining good public relations with parents and the community.

Special Qualities

able to understand the needs, abilities, and interests of youngsters
able to relate well with adults
appreciative of outdoor living
able to use sound judgment
physically fit
able to handle emergency situations
flexible
able to organize and direct the work of others

Education and Training

A bachelor's degree is always desirable. However, experience in planning and implementing outdoor living experiences, along with a camp director training course, are essential.

Salary Range

$600–$5,000 per camping season (usually six to nine weeks)

Places of Employment

Girl Scout camps
other youth agency camps
private camps

Coach

Out-of-Doors

Greta Hadley is a bit of a big sister, a teacher, and most of all a psychologist. She uses her human touch to relate to young people, her technical knowledge to perfect their skills, and her understanding of psychology to help them cope with growing pains. Greta Hadley is a coach in every sense of the word.

Greta, full-time teacher and part-time coach, particularly enjoys her coaching tasks. As she explains, "You get to know kids in a different way. You bring them together as a family." But it doesn't happen overnight.

Along the way there's lots of hard work, occasionally frustration, sometimes disappointment, and always pressure. As the season begins in November with tryouts, Greta faces an unpleasant part of her job—selecting 15 girls out of 100 for positions on the basketball team. Then, as preseason practices get underway, the hard work begins with drills and scrimmages. During this time, Greta supervises, analyzes, corrects, and encourages her players. She aims at improving skills, teamwork, confidence, and, most important, spirit.

Greta confides that she's nervous on the day of a game, but in order for her players to be in the right frame of mind, she tries her best to project a relaxed, cool image. But she says, "Underneath, I'm dying." Then, from the time of the tap, adds Greta, "I don't stop talking, I don't stop screaming." And when the game is all over, win or lose, she gets in her car, rolls up the windows, and screams as loud as she can. Then she goes home, exhausted and ready to unwind.

Despite the pressure, the frustration, the long hours, and little pay for part-time coaching, when you win, "it's an ego trip." And, she adds, "Win or lose, when the kids are satisfied with you as a coach, when you've given them your best and received the same in return, that's really what counts."

Coach

A school coach instructs students in the rules and skills of a sport. A coach demonstrates playing techniques, conducts drills in fundamentals, prepares players for competition, encourages good sportsmanship, assigns team positions, and plans game strategies. Coaches also work with Olympic teams and in professional sports.

Special Qualities
able to work well with others
interested in athletics
able to motivate others
physically fit
organized
emotionally stable
enthusiastic

Education and Training
School coaching positions are available to teachers with a bachelor's degree.

Salary Range
$300–$75,000+

Places of Employment
colleges and universities
professional teams
Olympic teams

Forester

Out-of-Doors

Keelin Reardon remembers planting holly trees with her Junior Girl Scout troop. An ordinary childhood memory for some girls, perhaps. But for Keelin, a professional forester, this experience had special meaning.

On an average day, Keelin might walk ten miles, sometimes fighting through thick brush, other times delighting her way through blueberry patches. Dressed in boots, a long-sleeved shirt, overalls, a hat, and coated with plenty of insect repellent, Keelin carries out her job marking trees and estimating their height, width, and number. Along the way, she is getting dirty, growing tired, and looking forward to rest, relaxation, and a hot shower at the end of her day. One summer she surveyed 25,000 acres of forest land like this, tagging 5,000 acres to be cut. Keelin explains that clearing trees improves the wildlife habitat and, in this case, the forest regenerates within 15 years.

Despite the bugs, ticks, dirt, and an occasional giant spider web, Keelin loves her job. "I go camping to enjoy the woods." Now, as a forester, Keelin enjoys the woods on the job, too. Getting to know an area well—the trees, the birds, the wildflowers—is particularly rewarding for her. Of course, there are times when the forest is strictly a workplace. Surveying land and shouting out tree measurements until her mouth is dry is hard work. When Keelin sees the forest as numbers, not nature, her job becomes a task, not a pleasure.

Keelin has some sound advice for aspiring foresters. According to her, you should be prepared to take a lot of science and math courses (including calculus), and be observant, healthy, and physically fit. And, most important, be able to cut it in the out-of-doors.

Forester

A forester manages, develops, and protects forests. She/he estimates the value of forest resources (timber, water, or wildlife); plans and supervises the cutting, purchase, and sale of trees; and makes suggestions for the marketing and use that follows. The job also involves protecting forests from fire, destructive insects, and diseases.

Special Qualities

healthy
hardy
appreciative of the out-of-doors
interested in science
concerned about ecology and conservation

Education and Training

A bachelor's degree with a forestry major is required.

Salary Range

$14,800–$50,000

Places of Employment

industries (pulp, paper, lumber, and logging companies)
U.S. Forest Service
colleges and universities

Horse Trainer

Out-of-Doors

When Judy Henvy was growing up, she always loved horses. In fact, she used to slip under the fence at a nearby raceway to pet the horses and give them sugar. Some twenty-odd years later, Judy still loves horses, pets them, and feeds them. But today, Judy Henvy doesn't have to crawl under a fence; it's her full-time job.

As a horse trainer, Judy begins her day at 6:00 A.M. cleaning stalls and scrubbing feed tubs. (She compares this part of her day to making a bed in the morning.) Then the training begins. One at a time, she brushes, harnesses, and jogs each of the four horses in her care. After this daily workout, each horse is bathed, warmed, walked, and brushed again. Their legs are bandaged and their feet are packed. As if this were not enough work, on those nights when one of her horses is entered in a late race, Judy may not return home until 2:00 A.M.

How does she keep up this rapid pace? "It's simple," Judy says, "it's not a job, it's a love." (And she does get an occasional helping hand from one of her five children.) Seeing one of her horses turn into the stretch brings Judy a special feeling. But she recognizes that horse training is a tough business. "In the winter, when the wind blows and it's freezing cold, there's no escape—you've got to get out and jog your horses." Then there are the damp barns and the late hours. It's Judy's feeling, however, that true animal lovers like herself can adjust to these less-than-comfortable conditions.

Any advice for an aspiring young horse trainer? According to Judy, who spent six years as a groom before becoming a trainer, you've got to love horses and like the outdoors. Also, because there is little formal schooling for grooms and trainers, you've got to start at the bottom, build experience, and work your way up. All of this, she adds, takes hard work—lots of it.

Horse Trainer

At a racetrack or a horse farm, a horse trainer conditions horses through workouts, bringing them to their best physical condition for competition. Usually, the horse trainer directs a staff of grooms and stablehands in the grooming, feeding, and care of horses. In other locations, a horse trainer's responsibilities vary. At a circus, for example, she/he may teach horses to perform tricks. Or, the trainer may prepare a horse to compete in a horse show.

Special Qualities

fond of animals
physically fit
appreciative of the out-of-doors
hardy

Education and Training

There are very few formal training programs. Most horse trainers learn on the job.

Salary Range

$5,000-$60,000+

Places of Employment

racetracks
horse farms
horse shows
circuses

Horticulturist

Out-of-Doors

As far back as she can remember, Melanie Menachem wanted to be an explorer. So, after graduating from college, she harvested her vegetable garden, gathered her plant books, packed her fishing equipment, and went exploring different plants around the country in a camper.

Today, as a horticulturist at a natural science center, Melanie is still exploring plants. Although she spends each morning "plantkeeping" (watering, propagating, transplanting, fertilizing, and pruning—all with tender loving care), the rest of her day is not so structured. She may devote her afternoons to planning demonstrations for visiting schools, arranging exhibits in the greenhouse, or, more likely, playing plant doctor for local people who bring in their sick specimens. Melanie recalls the time an elderly couple brought her a plant that had not been repotted in over 32 years!

Melanie is especially proud when she sees any type of seed or cutting take root, grow, and flower. But she regrets that the budget doesn't always allow for enough money to purchase fertilizer needed in the greenhouse. Despite this frustration, Melanie loves working with plants. In the future, she envisions a slight change of scenery—to a large botanical garden where she can concentrate on a cactus and succulent collection (her favorite!).

For girls who might want to enter this field, Melanie has some reminders. "This job is physical and by no means clean." Melanie further explains that she dresses for work in old clothes and expects them to be a shade darker at the end of the day. And then there are insects; "they can drive you out of your mind." But she concludes, "If you can survive all of this, you've got it made."

Horticulturist

A horticulturist is an expert in the growth and cultivation of flowers, vegetables, fruits, landscape plants, and nursery stock. The broad range of work in the field of horticulture includes developing new plant varieties and experimenting with ways to improve growing techniques. Some horticulturists may spend most of their time in research; others do conservation work (like planting trees), teach, or work in the area of garden care.

Special Qualities

appreciative of the out-of-doors
interested in plant life
able to work well with hands
able to work independently

Education and Training

The minimum requirement is a two-year technical program in horticulture.

Salary Range

$14,822–$35,400

Places of Employment

nurseries
landscaping firms
government agencies
colleges and universities

Meteorologist

Out-of-Doors

For meteorologist June Bacon-Bercey, there was no rain on her parade.

In her 15-year career as a meteorologist, June has been a prognosticator (making pictures of the atmosphere as it will look in 24-hour intervals); a forecaster (using the prognosticator's pictures to forecast weather in her locale); a television personality (reporting on science and the weather); an international aviation specialist (providing weather information to pilots of commercial airlines and small craft); and, most recently, an administrator (helping to design weather stations of the future).

Although June thoroughly loves her job, she's quick to admit that her steady climb up the career ladder meant compromising on excitement and fun for additional money and responsibility. Looking back, June recalls the fun of forecasting. And she rates "hitting her forecast" as her number-one reward. She claims that there is no greater thrill than seeing a storm develop, forecasting it, tracking it, and watching it hit.

But according to June, who compares forecasting to horseracing, you're not always right. As she explains, forecasting is not an exact science, and when you're wrong you must be able to bounce back. "You have to be thick-skinned in this job," she notes.

What about a woman in a male-dominated profession? (There are over 9,000 males and less than 200 females in the field of meteorology.) June confides, "I took the brunt of a lot of jokes." But what she finds most annoying is the occasional person who questions her knowledge as a meteorologist simply because she's female. June recalls one such time she responded to the captain of a ship headed for a storm. "I gave him the right advice, but he wouldn't take it!"

Meteorologist

A meteorologist studies the earth's atmosphere. Through analysis, prediction, and control of atmospheric phenomena, a meteorologist helps solve practical problems in business, industry, health, communications, and agriculture. Aircraft design, air pollution control, spacecraft reentry, and research into how diseases spread are some of the areas where progress has been made through the application of meteorology. Some meteorologists specialize in research; others choose weather forecasting; and still others work as educators, consultants, and administrators.

Special Qualities

curious about nature
interested in science
observant
able to handle complex scientific equipment

Education and Training

A bachelor's degree in meteorology is required.

Salary Range

$14,822–$45,000

Places of Employment

government agencies
colleges and universities
industries (aerospace, utilities, communications, and transportation companies)

Naturalist

Out-of-Doors

As a young child, Caryl Simon loved the out-of-doors. She treasured bird feathers, wildflower guides, and even seed catalogs. But most of all she cherished memories of sloppy slurching (walking through a creek, sneakers and all) at Girl Scout camp. Perhaps these interests explain why today Caryl Simon is so naturally a naturalist.

At a natural science museum, Caryl spends the winter months teaching about the natural environment. In the planning stage, she calls principals and PTA groups to arrange to bring her programs into the schools. Next, there's the preparation: gathering materials, organizing lessons, and visiting in advance the parks and natural areas where the activity will take place. Then she teaches the class, which may include blind-sense walks and how-to lessons on making wild salads or preparing natural dyes.

When school is out and spring turns to summer, Caryl leaves her outdoor classroom for her natural workshop. With a conservation crew of volunteer youngsters, Caryl builds nature trails, constructs boardwalks through swamps, and clears orchards of unwanted trees. As Caryl explains, this sort of work is far from clean. There's the mud, the insects, the snakes, and finally two hot showers when she returns home.

Although she thoroughly enjoys this physical side of the job, she prefers teaching. As she says, "Nothing equals a successful class." However, because she works with a group for only a short period of time and can't arrange follow-up sessions, Caryl doesn't always see results.

If you're interested in a career as a naturalist, here's some advice from a true wildflower person. "Get out and experience nature. If you like birds, get binoculars and a field guide and go birding. If you like wildflowers, go look for them. But better than that, go camping!"

Naturalist

A naturalist (or environmental educator) studies flowers, animals, geological formations, and other natural features of the land. This information is used to plan programs—exhibits, informal classes, field trips—to inform the public about the natural, scientific, and historical features of an area such as a community park.

Special Qualities

appreciative of the out-of-doors
skilled in oral communication
observant
hardy
friendly

Education and Training

A bachelor's degree in environmental science, geology, natural history, or a related field is required.

Salary Range

$10,000–$30,000

Places of Employment

national parks
community parks
natural science museums
youth organizations (such as Girl Scouts of the U.S.A.)
recreation centers

Park Administrator

Out-of-Doors

Jane Henzi claims that it was "just magic" that she was selected for the park ranger training program. But it took more than magic to attain the number-three position in a 26,000-acre national park.

How does Jane, who had never before seen a cactus, climbed a mountain, or packed a mule, account for her steady climb up the park career ladder? "I got programs going," reports Jane about her previous park experience. She recalls the living history program she started at a restored iron-making village, and the outdoor classroom she initiated. Today, after transfers (from Colorado to Pennsylvania to New York) and two promotions (from ranger to manager to assistant superintendent), Jane still has her hand in shaping programs, but now she is in charge of promoting them, too.

"It's not a 'get-dirty' job, it's a 'people-exchange' job," says Jane about her appointment as assistant superintendent of external affairs at the park. Much of her day is spent telephoning and meeting people to arrange press conferences and workshops designed to explain the park to the public. But planning strategies to promote the park's programs also involves a lot of letter and report writing. For Jane, turning people on to these park programs is the top reward. "Especially," she adds, "when they in turn spread the word for you." Frustration, on the other hand, results "when you thought you reached your audience, but they never really heard you."

If a park "people-exchange" position turns you on, Jane maintains that you must be able "to listen to people, not just hear them." And that's a skill that takes time to learn.

Park Administrator

The administrator of a park is in charge of the facility and coordinates the efforts of all park departments and staff in order to provide public services. The job involves managing personnel, facilities, and finances; planning programs; preparing a budget to meet current and future needs of the community; and dealing with the public.

Special Qualities
able to organize and direct the work of others
interested in the community
business-minded
creative

Education and Training
A bachelor's degree and previous park experience are required.

Salary Range
$20,000–$45,000

Places of Employment
national parks
community parks
state and local agencies

Recreation Leader

Out-of-Doors

Carla Sacco first became interested in horses by taking occasional trail rides. A few years later, her hobby grew into a weekly habit. And after her first horse show, she knew she was hooked.

"It's my first home," says Carla about the riding academy where she now works. Although Carla works only part-time, her full-time work as a student leaves her very little time at home. She's in college and an A student. On a typical day after school, Carla arrives at the stables about an hour before her students do to care for her horse. She grooms him, rides him, cleans him, and picks his feet. She usually instructs three classes on a weekday (more on weekends), ranging from beginner to lower advanced; from seven-year-olds to adults. During class time she teaches her students horseback-riding skills, and observes and analyzes her students as they ride for safety, position, and control. Between classes she conducts "privates," sessions when she works with individuals to help them polish their skills.

Carla is happy being around horses. "If I had a million dollars, I'd have all the horses I want." But she also likes teaching. In her words, "I like kids (I'm one myself), and I like feeling independent and important, too." Carla finds teaching disabled persons particularly rewarding. She tells of one girl with a coordination problem who is about ready to compete in a horseshow.

The only drawback, as she sees it, is time (or lack of it). Because she works on weekends, Carla can't go to horseshows as often as she'd like. But that won't be a problem for long. Carla is looking forward to the time when her students have progressed to the point where she can take them to horseshows so that they can demonstrate equitation skills.

In a happy atmosphere where no one voluntarily goes home ("they have to be pulled out," she says), Carla is understandably happy that she's attending a local college so she can continue her education (in animal husbandry) and her job, too.

Recreation Leader

A recreation leader plans, instructs, and supervises individuals or groups of all ages in activities such as arts and crafts, tennis, horseback riding, skiing, swimming, dancing, or gymnastics. The recreation leader often coaches teams in the sport in which she/he specializes.

Special Qualities

able to motivate others
physically fit
patient
able to communicate well
creative
resourceful

Education and Training

All positions require advanced skills in the area of specialty. For some positions, an associate's degree with a major in recreation is required.

Salary Range

$6,500–$20,000
(Many jobs are available only on a seasonal and/or part-time basis.)

Places of Employment

camps
youth organizations
resort hotels
community centers

Recreation Specialist

Out-of-Doors

According to Laurann Lundquist, she accidentally stumbled on her career in recreation. Or at least it seemed that way. But for Laurann, who has always been active in sports, camping, and every kind of student activity imaginable, pursuing a career in recreation was the natural thing to do.

Today, as a recreation specialist for a large county department of parks, Laurann plans countywide recreation programs. If, for example, a park concert is planned, Laurann selects and schedules the entertainment. She also promotes the event with local media, oversees the program while it is happening, and arranges to pay for all expenses with her limited county budget.

Laurann spends a good deal of her working time indoors, behind a desk. As she explains, "Coordinating countywide events requires a lot of talking, a lot of writing, and a lot of local travel, too." Outdoors, Laurann oversees the programs she spends months coordinating. That's when she feels like a hostess at a big party (sometimes hosting up to 10,000 guests!). "I can have a ball all day," she says, smiling, "but I'm still doing my job."

But not all of Laurann's work is pleasurable. There are frustrations, too. As she explains, "I'm a one-woman department." With no assistants, not even a secretary, Laurann often does what she calls the "rinky dink" things like blowing up balloons.

For anyone interested in this field, Laurann advises getting a college degree in recreation and gathering bits of related experience along the way. She adds that liking people is a must and a good memory runs a close second. "You can spend months coordinating a major event," she remarks, "but on opening day success means remembering the scissors for the county executive to cut the ribbon!"

153

Recreation Specialist

A recreation specialist plans, organizes, and directs recreation activities. These activities may be athletic, social, or cultural and are commonly held at parks, camps, hospitals, community centers, and other facilities. While some recreation specialists plan total recreation programs, others specialize in one area such as dance, drama, or environmental education. The recreation specialist must work closely with people from diverse businesses and organizations in order to coordinate events that will meet the needs and interests of the communities that are served.

Special Qualities
able to motivate others
creative
resourceful
outgoing
organized
detail-minded

Education and Training
A bachelor's degree with a major in recreation or in an area of specialization (such as drama or environmental education) is required.

Salary Range
$12,000–$30,000

Places of Employment
community recreation departments
resort hotels
schools
camps
youth organizations
community centers

Soil Scientist

Out-of-Doors

Since she was nine, Marilyn Cassidy has had an interest in farming. An ordinary sideline for a country girl, perhaps. But when you're born and bred in a big city?

Marilyn's fascination began when she enrolled in a gardening class at a botanical garden in her hometown. "I grew these huge tomatoes. People wanted to buy them from me on the bus ride home."

So it's not surprising to learn today that Marilyn has moved from the big city to rural America where she works as a soil scientist. On an average summer day, she walks about seven miles (through all kinds of terrain), digs three or four ditches (each about 3½-feet-deep), and bores close to 25 holes. This field work allows her to analyze, classify, and map different soils. Then, when summer ends, her work takes her indoors where she prepares maps and charts showing soil boundaries.

Marilyn, who especially enjoys the outdoors, has the advantage of bird watching and rock collecting on the job. But there are drawbacks, too. The summers are hot and humid and, according to Marilyn, "you sweat an awful lot." And the fields are loaded with deer flies, mosquitos, and poisonous plants. (And most frustrating for Marilyn is losing herself on the map.) But these are only part-time problems. While the job can be lonely in the summer (Marilyn works by herself, sometimes in acres and acres of undeveloped land), winter brings a welcome change of pace. "In the office," she says, "it's one big happy family and everyone works together."

If you're considering a soil science career, Marilyn has some down-to-earth advice. You have to be strong and physically fit. You can't expect to go to work (or come home) looking beautiful. And you have to feel free about moving quickly and often. As Marilyn explains, "Finish mapping one county, and it's off to the next."

Soil Scientist

A soil scientist studies characteristics of soils both in the field and in the laboratory and classifies the soils according to a national system. Based on this information, the scientist prepares maps plotting the different kinds of soils in an area. A soil scientist may be consulted on questions about land management. For example: Is the soil suitable for building? For growing crops? For planting trees?

Special Qualities

hardy
able to work independently
physically fit
appreciative of the out-of-doors

Education and Training

A bachelor's degree in soil science or a closely related field is required.

Salary Range

$14,800–$50,000

Places of Employment

colleges of agriculture
real estate firms
government agencies
fertilizer companies
state conservation departments

Sportswriter

Out-of-Doors

At 22 and fresh out of college, Robin Herman landed a job as a sportswriter on one of the largest newspapers in the country. But it didn't happen overnight. According to Robin, she had already been in the business for quite some time.

When she was only eight, Robin was using her toy printing press (the one with rubber letters) to put out a block newspaper. Later on, she wrote news articles for her elementary, junior high, and senior high school papers, and finally, the college paper and her introduction to sportswriting.

Today, Robin covers all her home team's hockey games, following the beat from Montreal to Moscow. (She even learned to speak Russian.) She begins a game day (three or four days a week) at noon "hanging around" practice, and interviewing players and coaches for a pre-game story and a 7:00 P.M. deadline. During the game, Robin sits in the press box watching the plays and writing a story at the same time. And after that, she's interviewing again for a final story and a 1:00 A.M. deadline.

Robin finds satisfaction in seeing her story in print the next day—especially if she has managed to capture the entire game in the limited space allowed. "It's like writing in a phone booth," she jokes. But, in a job that seems so glamorous, there are drawbacks too. Robin recalls the irregular weekends and odd hours.

What about a woman sportswriter on the hockey scene? At first, some people were outraged, others shocked, and still others amused. But today, Robin reports, "It's more of an ice breaker than anything else."

Sportswriter

A sportswriter reports on local and national sporting events, from high school to professional contests, for newspapers, magazines, television, and radio. The writer observes games and interviews coaches, players, and other people behind the scenes. She/he may write a running story describing the game play by play, a feature story, or a human interest article.

Special Qualities
interested in athletics
self-motivated
willing to travel
outgoing
able to write well

Education and Training
A bachelor's degree in journalism or a closely related field is required.

Salary Range
$19,300–$37,000+

Places of Employment
newspapers
magazines
radio stations
television stations

Zookeeper

Out-of-Doors

For a young woman who enjoys dining with an elephant and looks forward to returning home to a small apartment full of pets (three cats, a dog, and a starling missing a wing), Peta Rader's job as a zookeeper is not surprising.

Working with exotic animals may seem glamorous and exciting. But every morning Peta works in a dimly lit basement with broom, scrub brush, and hose in hand. Dressed in zoo shirt, pants, and water boots, Peta transfers the animals to display areas and then cleans their cages from the night before. "It's hard physical labor, all right," admits Peta. Peta adds that at the end of each morning her long hair is thoroughly soaked from perspiration.

Once her cleaning chores are behind her, Peta's work load lightens. Now she is free to spend time tenderly caring for the apes. Peta explains that gorillas have emotional needs in the same way children do. So it's not unusual to see her finger painting with two young male gorillas she calls her "boys." Nor is it surprising to hear them cry when she leaves their cages.

As for a woman on the job, according to Peta who stands five-foot-two and weighs 100 pounds, you have to like hard work and know how to handle animals. In her words, "Male or female, you can't force a 400-pound gorilla to move."

To a young girl interested in a similar profession, Peta advises trying it out first. According to her, not everyone can take hard labor or unpleasant odors. She recommends volunteering at a zoo, a kennel, or the ASPCA. "After all," she adds, "that's how I got started."

Zookeeper

An animal keeper feeds and cares for animals in zoological parks, aquariums, or circuses. Job responsibilities include cleaning exhibit areas and sleeping quarters, reporting sick animals, and helping to treat minor injuries or illnesses under the direction of a veterinarian. Some animal keepers also bathe and groom animals and answer visitors' questions.

Special Qualities
sensitive to animals' needs
conscientious
knowledgeable about animals
hardy

Education and Training
A bachelor's degree in biology is preferred. Experience in the field, however, can sometimes equally qualify an applicant.

Salary Range
$14,822–$40,000

Places of Employment
aquariums
zoological parks
circuses

_____
(name of career)

photograph

_____
(world)

(name of career)

Job Description

Special Qualities

Education and Training

Salary Range

Places of Employment

_____

(name of career)

Job Description
_____
_____
_____
_____

Special Qualities
_____
_____
_____
_____

Education and Training
_____
_____
_____

Salary Range
_____

Places of Employment
_____
_____

|photograph| (name of career)

○

(world)

_____

(name of career)

Job Description
_____
_____
_____
_____

Special Qualities
_____
_____
_____
_____

Education and Training
_____
_____
_____

Salary Range
_____

Places of Employment
_____
_____

photograph

_____
(name of career)

_____
(world)

_____
(name of career)

Job Description
_____
_____
_____
_____

Special Qualities
_____
_____
_____
_____

Education and Training
_____
_____
_____

Salary Range
_____

Places of Employment
_____
_____

photograph

(name of career)

(world)

_____

(name of career)

Job Description
_____
_____
_____
_____

Special Qualities
_____
_____
_____
_____

Education and Training
_____
_____
_____

Salary Range
_____

Places of Employment
_____
_____

(name of career)

photograph

(world)

_____

(name of career)

Job Description
_____
_____
_____
_____

Special Qualities
_____
_____
_____
_____

Education and Training
_____
_____
_____

Salary Range
_____

Places of Employment
_____
_____

(name of career)

Job Description

Special Qualities

Education and Training

Salary Range

Places of Employment

_____

(name of career)

Job Description
_____
_____
_____
_____
_____

Special Qualities
_____
_____
_____
_____

Education and Training
_____
_____
_____

Salary Range
_____

Places of Employment
_____
_____

[photograph]

_____
(name of career)

◯

_____
(world)

_____
(name of career)

Job Description
_____
_____
_____
_____

Special Qualities
_____
_____
_____
_____

Education and Training
_____
_____
_____

Salary Range
_____

Places of Employment
_____
_____

photograph

(name of career)

(world)

_____

(name of career)

Job Description
_____
_____
_____
_____

Special Qualities
_____
_____
_____
_____

Education and Training
_____
_____
_____

Salary Range
_____

Places of Employment
_____
_____

|photograph| (name of career)

◯

(world)

_____

(name of career)

Job Description
_____
_____
_____
_____
_____

Special Qualities
_____
_____
_____
_____
_____

Education and Training
_____
_____
_____
_____

Salary Range
_____

Places of Employment
_____
_____

	(name of career)
photograph	◯
	(world)

(name of career)

Job Description

Special Qualities

Education and Training

Salary Range

Places of Employment

|photograph| (name of career)

○

(world)

(name of career)

Job Description

Special Qualities

Education and Training

Salary Range

Places of Employment

_____
(name of career)

photograph

_____
(world)

_____
(name of career)

Job Description
_____
_____
_____
_____

Special Qualities
_____
_____
_____
_____

Education and Training
_____
_____
_____

Salary Range
_____

Places of Employment
_____
_____